UNDERSTANDING ANOREXIA NERVOSA

By

FELICIA F. ROMEO, Ed.D., Psy.D.

Clinical Psychologist
Assistant Professor of Education
Florida Atlantic University
Boca Raton, Florida

CHARLES C THOMAS • PUBLISHER
Springfield • Illinois • U.S.A.

Published and Distributed Throughout the World by
CHARLES C THOMAS • PUBLISHER
2600 South First Street
Springfield, Illinois 62717

© *1986 by* CHARLES C THOMAS • PUBLISHER
ISBN 0-398-05191-7
Library of Congress Catalog Card Number: 82-20815

With THOMAS BOOKS *careful attention is given to all details of manufacturing
and design. It is the Publisher's desire to present books that are satisfactory as to their
physical qualities and artistic possibilities and appropriate for their particular use.*
THOMAS BOOKS *will be true to those laws of quality that assure a good name
and good will.*

Printed in the United States of America
Q-R-3

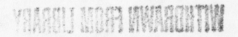
Library of Congress Cataloging in Publication Data
Romeo, Felicia F.
    Understanding anorexia nervosa.

    Bibliography: p.
    Includes index.
    1. Anorexia   nervosa. I. Title. (DNLM:
1. Anorexia Nervosa.   WM 175 R763u)
RC552.A5R66   1986   616.85'2   85-20815
ISBN 0-398-05191-7

UNDERSTANDING
ANOREXIA NERVOSA

To my mother and father,
Angeline D. Romeo and Paul C. Romeo
for their generous love, support, and encouragement

FOREWORD

SEVERAL YEARS AGO I found myself in a somewhat precarious circumstance. As a clinical psychologist, specializing in the treatment of eating disorders, I noticed an increasing number of patients were being referred to my office suffering from anorexia nervosa and/or bulimia. What has been thought of as an "obscure" or relatively "rare" syndrome was now becoming an epidemic. At that time, less than five years prior to this writing, little was known about these syndromes. Even more alarming, was the fact that with the exception of a few articles published in the professional literature, virtually nothing of value had been written on the subject. Needless to say, the available resources to treat these disorders were as scarce as the literature.

Many things have changed since then. For one, a growing number of treatment centers now exist which specialize in the diagnosis and treatment of anorexia and bulimia. The number of professionals able to treat these disorders has grown substantially. The professional literature now holds much promise in the way of research and which may eventually prove useful in our efforts to find more effective approaches to treatment. Families and professionals alike have joined forces and organized such non-profit groups as the National Association for Anorexia Nervosa Disorders and are able to inform and assist individuals and their families as well as provide support. All of these developments are encouraging.

Now, with the addition of Dr. Romeo's text, *Understanding Anorexia Nervosa*, another void has been filled. To date, there has not existed a straightforward text for the educator, family, clinician, or patient to read. *Understanding Anorexia Nervosa* offers a thorough review of anorexia nervosa and allows the reader to truly understand the nature of this syndrome. For the clinician, the book provides a practical guide to treatment. For the educator, it is an invaluable resource. For the family, it offers answers to questions ranging from cause to treatment. For the suffering, it gives direction and hope.

Dr. Romeo has clearly identified the questions and explained the answers for those most concerned by the problem of anorexia nervosa.

Martin E. Lerner, Ph.D.
Director
Humana Hospital Biscayne
Anorexia/Bulimia Treatment Center
Miami, Florida

PREFACE

THIS BOOK was written to help others understand the many dangerous aspects of anorexia nervosa. I feel fortunate that I have been granted the opportunity to make a contribution to the current literature. As a clinical psychologist, I have included information relevant to the dynamics of the illness as well as current treatment techniques. As an educator, I have organized the information in a way that could be understood by someone without a background in psychology. Together, we have a responsibility to try to change the social conditions which contribute to the expression of the disorder and to identify anorectics during early stages of the illness. This can only be accomplished by becoming informed and thereby taking appropriate action.

ACKNOWLEDGEMENTS

I EXTEND my thanks to the editors who gave me permission to use information from articles which I have written in the following journals: *Psychotherapy In Private Practice, Adolescence, Middle School Journal, The High School Journal, The Delta Kappa Gamma Bulletin,* and *The Physical Educator,* a publication of Phi Epsilon Kappa. Thanks are due to Martin E. Lerner, Ph.D., and Anne T. Patsiokas, Ph.D., for sharing with me their clinical expertise. A special thanks to Mrs. Nancy Mims for her skillful editing of the manuscript. I am extremely grateful to Mrs. Gloria Panoch for her patience, understanding and personal encouragement and for the many, many hours which she devoted to several revisions and final draft of the manuscript. I owe a debt of gratitude to my good friend, Carmen A. Morales, Ph.D., who read, edited and reviewed several drafts of the manuscript and made valuable suggestions for improving it. It was only due to her friendship and encouragement that I was able to go through the task of completing this book.

INTRODUCTION

THOUSANDS OF adolescent girls and young adult women are victims of anorexia nervosa, a life threatening mental illness. Anorectics are obsessed with thoughts of becoming "thinner" even when they are severely emanciated. They combine a severely restrictive diet with vigorous activity as they pursue "thinness." The incidence of anorexia nervosa has increased over the past twenty years. A review of the psychiatric case register in Monroe County New York, reported an increase in the incidence of anorexia nervosa from 1960-1969 to 1970-1976.[1] Hospital staff at the University of Wisconsin Hospital treated an average of one anorectic per year just twenty years ago. Now the hospital treats over seventy anorectics per year.[2]

The high risk age population for anorexia nervosa is adolescent females between twelve and eighteen years of age. Within this age group as many as one girl in 250 may develop the debilitating disorder.[3] The disorder affects a wider age range within the population as there are cases of anorexia nervosa reported before age ten[4] and even to age seventy.[5] Many young girls and women in our society are starving themselves and this self-starvation course may eventually lead to death. Mortality rates for anorexia nervosa are reported at 5%.[3] Recovery rates are even pessimistic: approximately two-thirds of anorectics recover while the others remain chronically ill.[6]

Anorexia nervosa is reaching alarming proportions in society; however, it is not a new disorder. Anorexia nervosa was mentioned in the medical literature as early as the seventeenth century. In 1694, Dr. Richard Morton, a London physician, wrote about young, wealthy females who were victims of self-starvation.[7] In the eighteenth century, anorexia nervosa was confused with tuberculosis, and later during the nineteenth century, it was diagnosed as a form of hysteria, a psychological illness. In the early part of the 20th Century, anorexia nervosa was considered to be the result of a pituitary disturbance and, therefore, an organic disease. In 1914, Dr. Simmond, an endocrinologist related the symptoms of anorexia nervosa to symptoms resulting from a destructive lesion of the pituitary gland. For the next twenty-five years, anorexia nervosa was diagnosed as Simmond's disease, a primary endocrine disorder.[8]

Today, anorexia nervosa is once again classified as a mental illness; specifically, an eating disorder. According to strict diagnostic criteria, the symptoms of anorexia nervosa include the following:

a) intense fear of becoming obese, which does not diminish as weight loss progresses
b) disturbance of body image, e.g., claiming to "feel fat" even when emaciated
c) weight loss of at least twenty-five percent of original body weight
d) refusal to maintain body weight over a minimal normal weight for age and height
e) no known physical illness that would account for the weight loss.[3]

Women account for 95% of the cases.[3] An estimated 1% of women in the United States, approximately 280,000, are victims of anorexia nervosa. Some believe the figure is even higher, and that anorexia nervosa afflicts at present more than half a million women.[9]

Men account for 5% of the reported cases. Anorexia nervosa in men closely resembles the condition in women. Men, however, have a reduction in the level of the hormone, testosterone, instead of amenorrhea.[10] One explanation for the lower incidence of anorexia nervosa in men is that they are not subjected to the same cultural pressures for thinness. The cultural standard of male attractiveness emphasizes muscularity, strength, and bulk. The ideal body shape for men is that of the muscle-bound athlete.

The incidence of anorexia nervosa has sharply increased over the past few decades. During this same time period, there have been significant cultural pressures for women to be thin, competitive with men, physically fit, and achievement oriented. These socio-cultural pressures contribute to the development of the incidence of anorexia nervosa among vulnerable women. The most significant social factor is the extreme amount of emphasis which the society places on dieting. For women in current society, dieting behavior is commonplace. At the same time, anorexia nervosa, a starvation illness, has received considerable attention from the popular press. Many women misuse information regarding the symptoms of anorexia nervosa and apply these symptoms to their dieting behavior. Instead of heeding the advice regarding the seriousness of the disorder, they regard anorexia nervosa as a successful dieting technique, an ideal method to lose weight quickly.

Many individuals demonstrate a casual attitude toward the illness. Comedians include jokes about anorexia nervosa in their performances. It is not unusual for a woman to laughingly say that she wishes she could have just a "little anorexia nervosa." A "little anorexia nervosa" does not exist just as a "little cancer" does not exist. Anorexia nervosa is an all or none process. Similar to cancer, it is a life or death situation. Although the victims of cancer lose a tremendous amount of weight in a short time, no one wishes for "just a little cancer" as an aid in losing weight. It is vitally important that anorexia nervosa, a mental illness, be given the same amount of regard for its dangerousness as we give to cancer, a physical illness.

Given that women represent a greater proportion of the anorectic population, this book will describe the illness as it relates only to women. It is written for parents and professionals who work with adolescents and young adult women as they share a collective responsibility in the early identification of potential anorexia nervosa victims. The book examines sociological, physiological, and psychological factors which contribute to the expression of the disorder among vulnerable adolescents. It describes the course of the illness and various medical and psychological treatment techniques.

Social values placed on slimness for women and the cultural emphasis on physical fitness and dieting serve to camouflage the anorectic's pathological behavior during the early stages of the illness. This book questions the current social values and attitudes which affect women and contribute to the development of anorexia nervosa. One of the most dangerous aspects of the disorder is that symptoms give the appearance of normal female adolescent behavior, particularly during the early stages. Consequently, the anorectic's behavior is not recognized as pathological. The book discusses the relationship between adolescent developmental issues and anorexia nervosa. The overall purpose of the book is to provide information to help in the early identification of potential victims of anorexia nervosa before the development of irreversible medical complications, and well before the loss of a young life.

CONTENTS

UNDERSTANDING
ANOREXIA NERVOSA

Chapter 1

COURSE OF ILLNESS

FAMILY BACKGROUND

ANOREXIA NERVOSA most often affects adolescent girls and
young adult women. The majority of anorectics come from families in the middle to upper-middle socio-economic class. Their fathers
frequently hold professional positions and their families enjoy all the
conveniences of modern living; they live in a fine neighborhood, and attend the best schools.

Many families of anorectics value physical fitness and they participate in some form of sports or physical activity on a regular basis.
Anorectics are often sport enthusiasts and they usually engage in a variety of sport activities. Their parents and coaches encourage and en-
dorse active participation in sports, and a few girls actually achieve
championship levels.[11]

The value of physical fitness and health carries over into the family's
eating behavior. One or both of the anorectic's parents will generally be
on a diet. Mothers and sisters of anorectics frequently have related eating disorders and place value on a slim appearance for all family members.[29] The entire family tends to be extremely nutrition and diet
conscious. Indulging in food for enjoyment is condemned, and family
topics of conversation often center around related health issues.

During her childhood the anorectic is described as a model daughter
who accepts all family values and tries to fulfill everyone's hopes and as-
pirations. She complies with the expectations of others and rarely dis-
plays any evidence of self-direction. At home she is cooperative, helps
around the house, and keeps her room well-organized. She is her
parents' pride and joy.

Her parents are generally highly educated and they place considerable value on academic achievement. In school their model daughter

demonstrates the qualities that teachers admire in their students. She complies with all the teacher's demands. Highly intelligent, she usually is placed in the advanced classes. She is extremely perfectinistic and self-critical toward her school work. Although she is self-motivated, her academic success often requires hard work and is attained only through considerable effort. She is extremely competitive, yet somewhat socially reserved, at times even shy. She usually relates well to her friends, but these relationships are often on a superficial level. She is neither interested in sexual topics, nor does she have a boyfriend.

SYMPTOMS BEGIN

The Diet

There is considerable disagreement in the literature concerning the pre-dieting weights of anorectics. In some studies anorectics are reported to be obese and overweight prior to their dieting behavior.[12] In other studies they are described as actually thin before starting their diets with only a small percentage considered overweight.[13] Many anorectics are within normal weight limits before they start their diets. Whatever their actual weight, they all perceive themselves to be too fat.

Anorectics often report that they started their dieting behavior following a particularly stressful event. Each anorectic reports a situation unique to her own circumstances and emotional problems. The precipitating event may be one of the following; sexual in nature, a separation from the family, or criticism about their body size. Whatever the specific event, the result for the anorectic is an increase in self-consciousness regarding her body and a loss of self-esteem.

The anorectic's initial decision to diet in order to improve her appearance is consistent with the family's value of a slim appearance. Although her weight may be within normal limits she receives praise and encouragement to diet from her friends and family. Anorectics generally begin by eliminating all carbohydrates, such as desserts, cakes and cookies from their meals. This is soon followed by reducing their intake of all high fat content foods. Additionally, the portion size of her meals is reduced which reduces the total calorie intake. Dieting becomes a major research topic as she seeks information on several different diet plans. During the initial stages of her dieting, the anorectic experiences hunger pains and frequently feels the urge to give in to her pains. Yet, she resists these moments of temptation and continues with her resolution to stay on her diet.

Amenorrhea

A major symptom of anorexia nervosa is amenorrhea, the cessation of menstruation. The actual onset of amenorrhea during the course of the illness varies among anorectics. Some anorectics report that the cessation of their menstruation occurred prior to any weight loss. Other anorectics report that their amenorrhea started after weight loss. Regardless of when, menstruation ceases for all anorectics some time during the course of the illness.[14] The anorectic does not demonstrate any concern over this event.

Hyperactivity

Anorectics are extremely energetic and engage in physical activities during the initial stage of the illness. Their hyperactivity appears to be a combination of involuntary and voluntary behavior. Hyperactivity may be the result of an involuntary discharge of internal tension or used as a conscious method of weight control. The anorectic realizes that by exercising additional calories will be burned, and, consequently, there will be a weight loss. Anorectics perform their exercises in a compulsive and ritualistic manner. They run or jog and will increase the distance for these activities on a regular basis. The anorectic considers exercising to be an essential part of her weight control plan.

Weight Loss

After some initial weight loss, the anorectic's friends and family compliment her on achieving a thinner shape. She begins to feel better about herself and to feel more confident about her appearance. She believes that if she continues with her diet and loses just a few more pounds, she will look even better. From past experience, she has learned that if she violates her diet plan by eating just a little more than she planned, her weight will increase. If, however, she stays on her current plan, she will only maintain her weight. She must, therefore, lower her total food intake even further to continue her weight loss.

THE PATHOLOGICAL SHIFT

During the initial stages of the illness, the anorectic's dieting behavior is undistinguishable from normal dieting behavior. At some unidentifiable point in the illness, however, her thinking becomes irrational and her dieting behavior becomes pathological. She becomes intensely fearful of gaining weight as she associates weight gain with being fat, gross, obese. Anorectics generally do not remember when this change occurred. Some report that they became aware of this fear after they had successfully lost weight.[15] From this point and during the course of the illness, the anorectic is extremely conscious of this fear, but she is unlikely to express it openly. She is more likely to say that she is too fat and needs to be thinner. Whenever the anorectic eats, she experiences high levels of anxiety. She cannot resume normal eating habits. She is caught in an internal trap which demands more and more weight loss. Thus, what began as a simple diet in order to lose just a few pounds is now an uncontrollable obsession.

After the pathological shift has taken place, and even though the anorectic has reached her initial goal for weight loss, she continues her diet. The turning point for her is the association of anxiety with eating. To control her anxiety, the anorectic engages in an even more restrictive diet. She categorizes foods as strictly "good" or strictly "bad." She refuses to taste even a small sample of these foods. Henceforth, calories are regarded as contaminants that must be strictly watched.

Hunger pains intensify. These severe pains conflict with her tremendous fear of eating and becoming fat. During this conflict some anorectics fight their urge to eat by mentally interpreting the hunger pain as a good sign of progress. Hunger pains are converted into a feeling of victory over fatness. From now on she knows that she is skinny whenever she feels the pain of an empty stomach. The anorectic enters into a contest with these hunger pains. She feels greater than human every time she conquers them. This feeling of triumph assumes considerable importance for the anorectic and raises her self-esteem. Anorectics rarely use diet pills or appetite suppressants to dull their hunger pains since without the pain, they would have nothing to defeat.

SYMPTOMS PROGRESS

Preoccupation With Food

Hunger and starvation cause the anorectic to be continuously preoccupied with thoughts of food. Her whole life becomes more involved and more organized around food. She may start a recipe collection and spend hours cutting, pasting, and copying hundreds of recipes. Hours are devoted to reading food magazines and gourmet cookbooks. Although she becomes extremely knowledgeable about food and nutrition, she is unable to use this information in a rational manner. She uses her calorie counting guide and becomes an expert in the exact amount of calories to be found in different foods. She keeps a daily notebook and records the number of calories in each parcel of food that she eats. The anorectic enjoys shopping for food in grocery markets, and spending hours gazing at food in shop windows. She particularly likes to buy and prepare food for others. She does not eat any of the prepared meal. The anorectic feels a sense of triumph as she watches others indulge while she abstains. In her mind she believes that if she abandons her diet, she will become ugly and obese. The anxiety and fear attached to this irrational thinking gains complete control over her behavior.

Hyperactivity

The anorectic is a young girl who is in perpetual motion. She is already an active person and involved in sports, but exercising has now become an obsession. The anorectic will increase her exercising especially after she has eaten one bite too many. She continues her exercise compulsion into the evening as well as during the day. She develops insomnia and also wakes up early in the morning. The disruption of her sleep pattern is associated with her eating less and exercising more. The anorectic continues to strive for perfection in her homework assignments. She begins to find, however, that it is more and more difficult to maintain her concentration on her school work. Thoughts of food constantly enter her mind. She may interrupt her homework to gaze at herself in the mirror, to weigh herself on the scale, or to do forty more sit-ups.

During the day she exercises for long periods of time without any apparent fatigue. Exercise helps her to combat severe hunger pains. At this point in the illness, the anorectic complains that she is full and her stomach aches after eating just a few bites. The anorectic's severe dieting behavior disrupts the functioning of her whole digestive system. She does not trust the sensations coming from her body which is biologically starved for calories. She fears that if she takes one bite, she may not be able to stop.

Weight Loss

The combination of excessive exercising and reduced caloric intake causes the anorectic to lose a substantial amount of weight. After she

eats her meager allotment for the day, she will immediately weight herself. Much of her time is now spent on the scale. She will look at herself
in the mirror for hours to assess the damages of a few crumbs. One day
she loses four or five pounds, and another day her weight remains the
same. Her moods fluctuate with the rise and fall of the numbers on the
scale. Each morning she will carefully inspect evey inch of her body for
fat tissue. In her own mind, she believes that she is too fat and that she
must stay on the diet. The anorectic is blind to the reality of her weight
loss. Even when she is extremely thin, well below normal weight, she
perceives herself as too fat. This distortion of her body image forces the
continuance of her destructive dieting behavior.

Pride

Along with the anorectic's pride on conquering her hunger pains, she
also is proud of her ability to lose weight. She has a feeling of ecstacy for
having so much control over her body. Every pound lost provides her
with a feeling of exhileration, accomplishment and specialness. Her thin
body gives her a unique identity all her own. Paradoxically, she takes
pride in her lean appearance, yet, she still regards herself as too fat.

THE FAMILY REACTS

The anorectic's parents begin to notice a determination in their
daughter's dieting behavior and become concerned about her weight
loss. They try to encourage her to eat, but she firmly insists that she
looks gross and fat. At mealtimes the anorectic and her parents have
painful confrontations over her dieting behavior. She gives them excuses
and tries not to eat her meals at the dinner table. Whenever possible, she
will bring her dinner to her room under the pretense of eating it there.
Instead of eating it, she will dispose of it. If the family meal contains any
foods of those on her forbidden food list, she will absolutely refuse to eat
them. She will also refuse to eat a full meal. Eventually, the anorectic
nibbles only a bite or two of food at very irregular times.

As her parents' worry mounts, they actively try to coerce her into eating. She meets their strength with her own display of stubbornness. The
more they try to force her to agree with their position, the greater is her
resolve and opposition. There are constant family arguments. Mealtime
becomes a battleground. When they try to stop her from exercising, she

responds with a violent outburst of anger. Her parents cannot understand the personality change which has taken place. She is far from the obedient child she used to be. She is now a stubborn and openly defiant girl regarding her diet.

The anorectic's parents try to explain to themselves the possible reasons for their daughter's negativism. They generally regard it as a sign of typical adolescent rebellion. Adolescents, the parents conclude, are trying to assert their individuality. Their daughter is also asserting herself, therefore, she must be going through an adolescent stage. They obtain additional reassurance by remembering that many of their friend's teenage daughters are also rebellious and are also dieting. These reassurances, however, are constantly challenged by their daughter's unyielding behavior.

The anorectic's parents are not aware of their daughter's internal conflict. Unknowingly, they are increasing their daughter's stress. The anorectic is trapped. She receives pressure from the family to eat, and she feels terror whenever she eats. Because of the desperation of her situation, she resorts to lying in order to reduce the parental pressure. From now on, nothing that she says with regard to eating will be true. She falsely declares that she has already eaten. She complains that she has lost her appetite and is not hungry. She will plead with them not to worry and to please leave her alone.

Her parents react to her lying by giving her severe warnings about her deceitful behavior. They judge her behavior to be deliberately malicious, and calculatingly hostile. They distrust her and constantly challenge her credibilitiy. They tell her that she "looks awful", and threaten punishment if she does not eat more. This punishment may be "grounding" her from pleasurable activities or taking away television privileges unless she gains a number of pounds.

ADDITIONAL SYMPTOMS

The Binge

For some anorectics the combination of family pressure, intense hunger pains, and a preoccupation with food, weakens their ability to maintain control over their dieting behavior and they binge (overeat). Anorectics define a binge as eating more than their calorie allotment for the day. Anorectics who live on a very low calorie diet, consider a binge as eating 100 calories over their limit. Others will consider a binge to be eating a large amount of calories within a very short time. Still others define a binge as eating moderate amounts of food but eating continuously throughout the day. The perception and definition of a binge rests within each individual anorectic.

The initial occurance of binge behavior varies among different anorectics. Some find it very difficult to stay on their diets and binge quite early in the course of the disorder. Others start their binge behavior at a much later time in the illness. Generally, the anorectic will binge on her favorite foods: foods which she has been depriving herself from eating. These foods can be very nutritious or foods with low nutritional value. There are those anorectics, however, who resort to more bizarre binge behavior, such as looking through garbage cans in the middle of the night.

Binging represents a loss of control over their eating behavior and this is frightening for the anorectic. Some anorectics fear that once they start eating they will not be able to stop themselves. This fear is related to their binging episodes and their inability to recognize the sensation of fullness. Consequently, most anorectics keep themselves extremely thin so that they can have a "margin of safety" should they lose control and binge.

Vomiting

There is considerable variation among anorectics as to the start of their vomiting behavior. Although some anorectics vomit early in the illness, others may never resort to vomiting. Those who do vomit may have learned to use self-induced vomiting as a result of watching a television program describing eating disorders. Other anorectics experience nausea after eating and vomit involuntarily. Afterwards, they recognize that the rapid removal of food reduced their feelings of anxiety. Henceforth, they use self-induced vomiting as a voluntary technique. Eventually, whenever the anorectic is forced to eat, she will secretly run to the bathroom and vomit. Once the anorectic begins vomiting behavior, she usually resorts to it for the duration of the illness. Many anorectics resort to self-induced vomiting after they have binged. Paradoxically, the anorectic is disgusted by her vomiting behavior, yet lengthy hours are spent in the bathroom trying to force food out of her stomach.

Purge

Besides vomiting, anorectics usually reduce their liquid intake as well as their food intake. Others, however, substitute only diet soft drinks for food, and drink considerable amounts of soda instead of eating. After drinking, some anorectics will use diuretics to eliminate fluid as a fast way to drop weight. The fluctuations in their liquid intake disturbs the anorectic's body water regulation system. Another means of reducing weight and eliminating food is through the use of laxatives. Anorectics consume small amounts of food and liquids, consequently, they suffer from chronic constipation. Their digestive tract slows down considerably. They may turn to laxatives in order to relieve their constipation. Anorectics also resort to laxatives whenever they are in a social situation which does not provide an opportunity for vomiting.

Laxatives speed the food through the digestive system, thereby increasing the anorectic's weight loss. In addition, the anorectic believes that the use of laxatives will flatten her stomach. Eventually, the anorectic develops a laxative dependency. The degree of laxative use can vary from eight to ten tablets every two weeks, to as much as daily doses of ten to twenty tablets in one month.[16] When the anorectic adds the techniques of vomiting and purging as part of her weight control plan, she gains the freedom to eat more without the consequence of weight gain. This leads her into a binge/vomit/purge cycle of behavior.

Binge/Vomit/Purge Cycle

When she loses control and overeats either a little or a substantial amount, she begins to feel extremely anxious. Her anxiety reaches such a level that she must vomit and/or take laxatives. Following this experience, she feels considerable self-loathing and guilt about her vomiting and purging behavior. The anorectic also feels less anxiety as she has eliminated her food. She then feels free to eat more, and the cycle begins again. The anorectic is trapped and helpless in this vicious cycle.

THE FAMILY SUFFERS

Towards the end stage of the disorder there are dramatic family scenes and constant arguments. The anorectic is caught between her parent's pleas and her fear of eating. She may run from the dinner table to cry in her room. The family gathering at mealtime is completely disrupted by the anorectic's irrational eating behavior. She begins to control the entire family. There are daily quarrels with her mother over who has authority in the kitchen. The anorectic always wins. Her family believes that giving in to her wishes will make her eat. Her parents buy food she likes and search for special foods. Even with these efforts, the anorectic will refuse to eat and accuse the family of purchasing the wrong variety or the wrong brand. Her parents are not the only ones who suffer. Siblings receive less attention as the whole family is controlled by the anorectic's eating problem. The anorectic's attitude toward them can be extremely critical. She keeps them under constant observation and criticizes their eating behavior: they are eating the wrong food, not she. At the same time she is highly sensitive to any criticism about her own eating behavior.

Every day the parents experience worry, fear, and apprehension. What should they do? Should they ignore her? Their lives revolve around the anorectic's life. The family is afraid that whatever they do will trigger a temper trantrum, thus they feel powerless to stop her destructive dieting behavior. In contrast to her parents' feelings of helplessness, the anorectic feels quite powerful. Her starvation attracts considerable attention, and she discovers that she has an effective manipulative tool. The anorectic's parents feel the control that their daughter has over them. Their emotions fluctuate with her weight fluctuations. Their hopes rise as she gains weight and fall when she loses weight.

One week she gains two pounds; the next week she loses six pounds. Eventually, the anorectic's parents lose all patience with their daughter and her refusal to eat. They feel defeated, humiliated, and insulted. As they realize their ineffectiveness at changing her behavior, their fear turns to anger and resentment. The parents become even more intrusive by threatening and coercing her to eat. They make rules, rewards and punishments. They threaten to put her in the hospital if she loses one more pound. She will not watch television for one week unless she gains a few pounds. Other times, they protect, beg, implore, or cajole her to eat. Everything they try, however, is met with failure. One thing angers the parents more than anything else: the anorectic's insistence that she is too fat. Her behavior is clearly irrational. They cannot believe that she is unaware of how dangerously thin she is. The anorectic's distortion of her body image is the most frustrating symptom for family members to understand.

Each night the anorectic's parents meet secretly in their bedroom to plan a strategy to induce their daughter to eat. They argue among themselves as they try to agree on one method. They are faced with the problem of trying to feed a starving child who defies all of their efforts. A common strategy used by parents is to force the anorectic to sit and eat her meals at the dinner table. Parents work out a schedule whereby they will take turns watching her eat. The mother watches the anorectic eat lunch; both parents supervise dinner. Unfortunately, the anorectic is forced by her mental illness to combat her parent's attempts at making her eat. She becomes skillful at appearing to eat. She pretends to eat when in reality she just moves the food to different corners of the plate. She may even cooperate and actually eat the meal. Later, she will either vomit or take extra laxatives.

The anorectic's parents worry extensively about their daughter. All other concerns and other family problems are pushed into the background. The anorectic child is their only priority. Her health and life take precedence over marital, financial and any problems with the other children. The whole family focuses on the anorectic. During this time of increased tension, family patterns of interaction may change markedly. The fathers may withdraw from the family and stop interacting with their daughters. Mothers often become the dominant parent in trying to change the anorectic's behavior.[21].

SYMPTOMS WORSEN

Bizarre Eating Behavior

Many anorectics eventually develop bizarre eating behaviors. Some ritualistically organize food on their plates while others cut food into little bits and then chew on the tiniest bites for hours. For example, in order to stretch their food, they will cut a raisin in half so that they will have two bites. Then they will chew on each half of the raisin forever.[18] They use large amounts of low calorie mustard, spices and salts, and they mix those items together on a lettuce leaf. At this stage, the anorectic has lost any sense of reality with regard to eating behavior and food.

Hunger and Satiety

Anorectics report during the later stages of the illness that they no longer feel hunger pains. The anorectic's chaotic eating pattern has destroyed her body's internal signals with regard to appetite. She is truly "anorexic" at this stage and has lost her appetite. Food restriction and malnutrition begin to take their toll on her body and health. The lack of appetite does not induce her to eat. She also states that she does not want to eat because food tastes bad to her. Although she may not complain of hunger, she may complain of feeling dizzy after she has eaten. Her whole digestive system is completely disorganized. She complains about stomach aches, nausea, and indigestion after eating just a small amount. Her stomach always feels bloated and she notices that her abdomen protrudes. She uses these complaints to fortify her belief that she is too fat.

Hyperactivity

At the end stages, the anorectic cannot continue with vigorous physical activity. Although she is extremely thin, she still feels a need to be constantly on the move. Her muscles become too weakened from the lack of nourishment to maintain her exercise plans. While her hyperactivity lessens, her overestimation of her body size still remains. The anorectic believes that she is too fat, even after losing twenty percent of her body weight. She cannot see the danger ahead.

Withdrawal

The anorectic gradually withdraws from her friends and her family. She becomes extremely uncomfortable whenever she eats in the presence of others. This situation eventually reaches such severity that she refuses to eat with her family or anyone else. She will eat only when she is alone and unobserved. She does this because she realizes that others ask questions about her eating behavior. Eventually, her eating behavior becomes a mystery to others. She is unable to tolerate any critical remarks about her eating behavior. The anorectic will not honestly reveal when she has eaten last or how much she has eaten. Other people represent a threat to her ability to maintain control; she feels safe only when she is alone.

The anorectic is at the mercy of external information to judge her weight. Because she regards herself as overweight, she is often surprised that her clothes are too big. If she is shopping, she is amazed to discover that she can wear a smaller size than she expected. The anorectic also relies on her scale as a source of information, and verifies her weight loss by weighing herself several times during the day. The anorectic's inability to recognize her emaciation contributes significantly to the seriousness of the illness. She is blind to the reality of her physical condition, and therefore, she is powerless to stop her dangerous dieting behavior.

The effects of the anorectic's behavior become more adverse. She no longer socializes with her friends. She wants to control others just as she controls her body. Her friends will not tolerate her dominating and controlling behavior and finally they withdraw from her. Eventually, she loses all of her school friends and is taken further away from any relationships. As the anorectic loses weight, she begins to wear bulky and layered clothes. This wearing of bulky and layered clothes not only hides her weight loss so as not to provoke questions, but also keeps her warm. In the later stages her body temperature is constantly below normal and she becomes highly sensitive to cold, or only slight cool temperatures. In addition to feeling cold, she suffers physical changes associated with malnutrition, such as dizziness and digestive problems. Her abnormal eating pattern and the frequent vomiting and purging have finally taken their toll.

Chapter 2

SOCIAL INFLUENCES

SOCIAL CLASS

HISTORICALLY, women have been modifying their bodies into various shapes in order to achieve the cultural standard of beauty. In the 19th Century women who were delicate and fragile in appearance were considered beautiful. During the Victorian period the whalebone corset forced every woman's body into the perfect hourglass figure. For some women the corset was responsible for displacing their internal organs. Other women had their lower ribs removed surgically in order to achieve the hourglass figure.[19] Today's woman alters her body by dieting to achieve a thinner appearance, society's current standard of beauty.

Weight and appearance are critical values in the socialization of young women in the upper classes. The results from a review of the Monroe County Psychiatric Register conducted in Monroe County, New York, revealed that the disorder most often occurs in the higher socio-economic level.[1] Ironically, woman who live amid comfort and luxury are most afflicted with a disorder associated with starvation. A study reported an inverse relationship between obesity and social class of women. Upper class women perceive themselves to be overweight when, realistically, they are not.[20] Cultural pressure toward female thinness, particularly in this social class, plays a major part in the formation of the disorder.

THIN WOMEN

Over the last twenty years the ideal shape promoted for women is "thin." Glamour magazines convey the message that a relationship exists

17

between popularity and being thin. For example, women pictured in *Playboy* and *Playmate* magazine centerfolds have become progressively thinner from 1959 to 1978. Since 1970 contestants in the Ms. America contest have become consistently thinner.[21] The actual average weight of women in the general population, however, has risen several pounds from 1959-1978.[21] Therefore, the ordinary woman is faced with a wide discrepancy between her actual weight and the weight which the beauty pageants represent as ideal.

In general, anorexia nervosa is found in greater frequency in those professions which place an emphasis on physical beauty and a thin appearance. Models on the covers of glamour magazines are often victims of anorexia nervosa. The conditions of their employment as well as their opportunity for employment depend upon maintaining a low body weight. Dancers as well as fashion models are under social pressure to be thinner. Consequently, the incidence of anorexia nervosa is over-represented in dance, particularly ballet, and in modeling students.[21]

The media selects only glamorously thin models to sell products. In 1977 trained raters observed prime time television shows, and they did not find any heavy women in continuing roles.[22] Gaunt models in fashion magazines represent the ideal female body. Fashions during the last two decades have been designed for the slim woman. Woman identify with these models; they wish to have thin bodies, an important factor in the development of anorexia nervosa. Victims of anorexia nervosa seek a thin silouette to achieve the "happiness" portrayed in the world of glamour.

FOOD

Although there are social pressures to be slim, women receive constant stimulation from the media to eat. On the one hand women are told that thin is beautiful, and on the other hand they are the prime audience for television gourmet cooking programs. Women prepare family meals and are the major consumers of food in grocery markets. Many social gatherings and professional meetings involve food. Food is frequently used as a reinforcer, a reward for hard work. Individuals are also more conscious of the nutritional value of food in our culture. People are concerned about preservatives and the shelf life of food. At the same time there has been a proliferation and acceptance of junk foods and fast food chains. Food is ever-present in our affluent society. Women are torn between two opposing forces: the stimulation to eat and constant pressure to be thin.

OBESITY

Social pressures favor obesity as much as they do slimness. Overeating is a common reaction to media cues and psychological cues. Over 30% of adult women in our society weigh at least 20% in excess of their ideal body weight and are, therefore, considered obese.[23] The prevalence of obesity increases according to the woman's age. For women in their twenties, the incidence is 12%; while for women in their fifties, the incidence is 46%.[23] Obesity is associated with serious health conditions such as cardiovascular disease, hypertension, diabetes and respiratory problems. Health professionals have spurred social campaigns to educate the public concerning the dangers of obesity. While individuals can survive with a 200% increase in body weight, they are in danger of dying with only a 25% loss in lean body tissues.[24] The social attitude toward the obese woman is one of disgust and shame. Society blames individuals for being fat. There is a prevailing belief that obesity is simply a result of overeating. Any woman who deviates from the stereotyped thin figure is considered gluttonous and weak. Thus, social pressures toward obesity carry negative and moralistic implications.

DIETING

Society's scorn for obesity and the value placed on a glamorous figure are the motivating factors for women to diet. Once again, the published media plays an important role. Six major women's magazines were reviewed for the number of dieting articles which they published during the past twenty years. In the first ten years there were 17.1 diet related articles. In the second decade, the number increased significantly to 29.6 articles on the subject of dieting.[25] The dieting industry has proliferated the marketplace with low calorie diet foods and food fadisms. Diet books are consistently on the national best sellers lists. For example the *Dr. Atkins Diet Book* was on the *New York Times* best seller list for forty-eight consecutive weeks.[26]

Women spend thousands of dollars on commercial diet aids, and wealthy women, additionally, spend weeks at expensive weight reducing salons. Weight control methods and dieting are constant preoccupations of a large number of American women. The dieting and thin-is-beautiful campaign have been so successful that 45% of all homes in the United States have somebody in the family who is dieting. Of all women dieting, 76% reported that their dieting was motivated by cosmetic rather than health reasons.[25] An overwhelming number of women in our society consciously restrain themselves from eating all the time.

PHYSICAL FITNESS

Women are also engaging in strenuous physical activity to reduce their weight. The Education Amendment Act of 1972, Title IX, provided women with equal opportunity in intercollegiate athletic programs. One result of Title IX is that athletics and sports form a greater part of the current female's educational curriculum. Educational principles provide national sanctions for participation of girls in physical fitness programs and, more importantly, to use exercising as a weight control technique.

The recent growth of the diet and physical fitness industry gives further support for the cultural value placed upon being thin. Fitness is packaged into products, wearing apparel, and video tape programs. Journals will devote entire issues to physical fitness themes. Physical fitness is one of the fastest growing industries in the country. Television physical fitness programs are regularly scheduled and receive tremendous ratings. Women of past generations relied more exclusively upon dieting behavior in order to lose weight. Today, society not only encourages, but advises women to combine physical exercises with their diet whenever they decide to lose weight. A woman's natural fat compositon is 20% of her body weight but today's athletically thin woman may have as little as 8% fat in her body weight.[19]

MEN

Men play a major role in the development of anorexia in women. Women diet and participate in physical fitness programs in order to be attractive to men. The popular view of the ideal female body is determined by the expectations of males in the society. She is constantly being appraised by men, and her future depends upon how she is seen, especially by men. Since she is not the glamorous beautiful thin ideal, she must be unattractive and, therefore, must change her body shape.

The culture encourages women to be vain regarding their appearance instead of their accomplishments. Women are either very proud or very insecure about their bodies. Fat is ugly, and thin is attractive. Women are encouraged to see their physical imperfections. Everywhere a woman turns, she is confronted with images of the perfect female form; in drugstores, supermarkets, and at cosmetic counters. She is constantly reminded that her figure is far from the ideal. Overall, she tries to change herself into a perfect thin shape by starving herself and by doing hundreds of painful exercises. Unfortunately for those women who develop anorexia nervosa, these cultural values of diet and exercise are taken to extremes.

WOMEN'S LIBERATION MOVEMENT

The recent expansion of the Women's Liberation Movement has had enormous cultural influence upon the role of women in our society. Such national women's issues as the Equal Rights Amendment and Affirmative Action have placed considerable emphasis upon women to achieve equal status with men. As a result, many women are encouraged to compete more with men and to strive for achievement through advancement in their professional careers. Heightened competitiveness and an over-evaluation of achievement are personality characteristics found among patients with anorexia nervosa.

The admission of women to traditional male professions (medicine, law, universities) has created additional pressures. Women were previously confined to the home in the role of mother and housewife. Now women are expected to compete and excel in business, as well as to spend time on their personal appearance. This emphasis on increased competitiveness extends to their dieting and to their appearance. Professional women of today are the first generation to be weight and exercise conscious. They are products of the social values of the 1960s, and their ideas of beauty are passed on to their daughters. Together mothers and daughters try to change their bodies through aerobics, jogging, and dieting. There may even be competition between them.

TODAY'S WOMAN

Over the past two decades there have been considerable changes in our culture which have contributed to the increase in incidence of anorexia nervosa. Anorexia nervosa must be viewed within the framework of socio-cultural conditions, as forces within the society directly influence the course of this mental illness. Today's teenage girl is bombarded by a host of cultural and social pressures in addition to her internal emotional pressures. She lives in a culture where the roles for women are more complex, changing, and conflicting.

The emphasis placed upon women to have a thin appearance and to be physically fit are additional contributing social pressures. Social conditions and the forces of media aid in the development of two of the major symptoms of anorexia nervosa: diet and exercise. The values of a culture are important factors to the mental health of the individuals living in that society. Symptoms of any mental illness are extreme exaggerations of behaviors which are regarded as normal behaviors by that culture. Our common social value system teaches that reducing will make one worth of love, beauty and happiness. The anorectic is seeking happiness by her dieting and exercising, and she jeopardizes her life in the process.

The anorectic has extremely low self-esteem which she tries to change by changing her body size. She wants to be accepted by others, and, therefore, she conforms to what society considers beautiful. This protects her from feeling different and gives her a sense of belonging. It reduces the expectation of criticism from everyone and she regards it as a solution to her painful feelings of low self-esteem. Cultural biases and social conditions, however, do not cause anorexia nervosa. Many girls who live in the same society and who experience the same social pressures do not develop anorexia nervosa. Sociological factors only contribute to the expression of the disorder in vulnerable girls, particularly adolescents.

What is there about adolescence that could explain the high incidence of anorexia nervosa in this age group?

Chapter 3

ADOLESCENCE

THE SYMPTOMS of anorexia nervosa manifest themselves during young adolescence or young adulthood. Anorectics generally report that the onset of their illness occurred during their adolescence. The high risk age range for anorexia nervosa is between twelve and eighteen years. There are reports of one severe case in two hundred below the age of sixteen, and one in every one hundred between the ages of sixteen and eighteen.[27] The high incidence of the disorder among adolescent girls suggest that developmental pressures inherent in adolescence are associated with the onset of the disorder. The development stresses of adolescence which are particularly relevant to anorexia nervosa are: rapid physiological changes which occur during puberty, psychological tasks of achieving autonomy from her family, and establishment of a female sexual identity.

PHYSICAL CHANGES

Latency precedes adolescence in the development sequence as the individual progresses toward maturity. The most impressive feature of the latency period is the physical similarity between the two sexes. In preadolescence boys and girls resemble each other in physical appearance and size. They have the same percentage of muscle and fat in their body composition, and they are similar in their fat distribution and skeletal shape.[28] The range of individual differences which are observable in latency is considerably smaller than in adolescence. More importantly, the amount of social attention given to their physical differences is considerably less than during adolescence.

In contrast to the similarity of physical appearance during latency, there is a dramatic difference in the physical appearance of adolescent

23

boys and girls. There are two developmental periods in which there is rapid physical growth: early childhood and adolescence. The adolescent growth spurt begins about two years earlier in girls than boys. Girls begin to grow more rapidly just prior to their entry to puberty, between ten and twelve years of age.[29] Between early and middle adolescence, the changes in growth are staggering. During this time adolescents will add the final twenty-five percent to their adult height and as much as fifty percent of their final adult weight.[28]

Secondary Sex Characteristics

Puberty is associated with the appearance of the adolescent's secondary sex characteristics. Girls notice an increase in fat distribution around their hips. They experience rapid changes in their height, weight and general body shape. The changes in girls' body weight are particularly striking. Females reach puberty early and, therefore, a large number of females will be fatter than their male classmates. Most girls will begin to form deposits of fat tissue just prior to puberty. During this time of rapid physical changes, adolescents are preoccupied and extremely self-conscious about their body image. They are sensitive to the differences between their own bodily changes and the physical changes of their peers. It is a time when a casual comment can be grossly exaggerated and cause considerable emotional distress. In locker rooms and slumber parties adolescents are constantly comparing their rate of development to that of their peers. The desire to conform is particularly strong during adolescence. Being different from others is being inferior.

OBESITY

Children learn stereotyped attitudes toward obesity early in their development. They regard being thin as good, and being fat as bad. The incidence of obesity varies in childhood from three to twenty percent.[24] The child learns directly or vicariously that to be fat is to be ostracized. Strong negative attitudes and even hatred toward obese children by other children and adults is apparent during latency. For example, one study found that children overwhelmingly preferred thin rag dolls over fat ones.[22] Prospective parents judged drawings of chubby children as less friendly and more stupid, dirtier, and less likeable.[22] These negative attitudes toward obesity form the foundation for self-hatred among children who become overweight during adolescence.

The incidence of obesity in adolescence ranges from ten percent to thirty-five percent of the population,[24] and obesity represents fifteen to twenty percent of the medical problems of adolescents.[28] Obesity is found more frequently among adolescent girls. Girls who are obese experience devastating social rejection from their peers. The topic of obesity is included in the curriculum of many high school subjects. Physical education, health, science, and home economics classes devote a portion of their curriculum to obesity and weight control. In these classes, teachers are likely to stress the medical problems as well as social handicaps associated with obesity. Adolescents are taught in high school to fear obesity as a danger to their health.

DIETING

The adolescent girl's attitude toward her body changes are related to her knowledge of the medical hazards of being obese as well as to her awareness of the social definition of a thin body. Obviously, there is a social handicap in the experience of the girl who deviates from cultural expectations. There are more social pressures on the adolescent girl to be fashionable and thin, and a greater social liability if she is overweight. The adolescent girl wants to minimize her shape. Many adolescent girls associate their pubertal changes with being fat and start dieting unnecessarily. A New England high school study reported that over sixty percent of girls started diets before they were seniors in high school.[30]

Adolescents need an increase in energy to support the rapid physical growth spurt. The nutritional needs of the adolescent are markedly increased. In particular, the adolescent girl has an increased need for iron in her diet because of menstruation. As a result of the rapid physical changes occuring during adolescence, her caloric need is greater than that of an adult female. The adolescent girl's nutritional requirement is in direct oppostion to society's pressure for a thin female body. Consequently, the teenage dieter sacrifices her nutritional needs as she seeks the socially valued thinner appearance.

Adolescents are more concerned about their body image and attractiveness rather than their nutritional needs. Consequently, many adolescent girls deliberately diet and eat less. Adolescents, in general, have poor and sometimes erratic eating patterns. Their main diet may consist of candy bars and potato chips. Even the "normal" adolescent female eats in an irregular manner. Some adolescents place such fear in obesity that they often engage in food fads and crash diet plans which cause considerable fluctuations in their body weight.

PSYCHOLOGICAL TASKS

In addition to adjusting to their rapid physiological changes, adolescents also need to master several psychological tasks as they progress toward maturity. Some psychological tasks hold particular relevance for the development of anorexia nervosa. These tasks include independence from their parents and establishing a female sexual identity.

Autonomy

Adolescents must face separation from their parents in their search for autonomy and independence. Many adolescents struggle with conflicting emotions as they search for autonomy from their parents. The storm and stress of adolescent rebelliousness conveys the adolescent's intense internal struggle and turmoil. They vacillate between a desire for the continuance of parental protection and a desire to conform with societal expectations for more independent functioning. In their efforts to separate from parents, adolescents adopt behaviors which are in opposition to their parents' wishes.

One way to demonstrate their independence and also to rebel against their parents is to alter their eating habits. Mealtime is often chosen as a way to loosen the family ties. Instead of eating with the family, adolescents choose to eat with their friends. As they strive for autonomy, adolescents shift their allegiance from their family to their peers. They identify with their own youth culture and reject traditional foods and diets. This rejection represents a statement of their individuality.

Sexual Identity

Another psychological task for adolescents is the establishment of a sexual identity which, in turn, leads to intimate heterosexual relationships and further separation from their parents. During adolescence, development of secondary sex characteristics create a sharp division between the sexes. Adolescents face the necessity of establishing their respective male and female roles in the society. The Fel's Institute large scale longitudinal study clearly supported the finding that during adolescence the issue of sex role assumes compelling power over the individual.[31] Adolescents experience strong sexual tensions and frequently report fears about masturbation, menstruation, and homosexuality. Hormonal changes increase the adolescent's awareness of sexual powers, fertility, sexual behavior, and interpersonal sexuality.

At puberty, adolescents confront the developmental task of integrating their body image with their respective male and female sex roles. The adolescent girl must integrate her physiological changes, menstruation, breast development, and fat distribution into a female sexual identity. The adolescent girl's pride is attached to her figure and face. Adolescent girls are also dependent upon their relationship with others in order to develop their female identity. The basis of their identity is interpersonal, and they rely on the opinions and reactions of others as they develop their female identity. Acceptance by peers is critically important for adolescent girls; they adhere strictly to peer group fashions, fads and idols.

Society provides the attributes and characteristics deemed representative of the female role. The adolescent girl internalizes these characteristics as she defines her role in society. For the contemporary adolescent this task is extremely difficult as the female role is changing within our society. Society's message concerning the qualities of femininity are mixed and confusing. De-coding society's message in an effort to establish a female identity is one of the most stressful psychological tasks facing adolescent girls today.

REGRESSION OR PROGRESSION?

Adolescents are pulled between two opposing forces: either to face the challenges of adolescence and progress toward adult maturity, or to regress and preserve their childhood dependency status. Many adolescents take the developmental tasks of adolescence in stride and proceed forward toward adult maturity. Other adolescents try to escape the pressures of adulthood through alcohol, drugs, or even suicide. The anorectic escapes into mental illness and uses food to avoid maturity and adult responsibility. The cause of anorexia nervosa and of any mental illness is the meaning which particular situations and events hold for the individual. The anorectic is frightened by the developmental tasks of adolescence: she tries to halt her forward development through dieting and regress to the protective status of her childhood.

SYMPTOM FORMATION

The anorectic experiences overwhelming and intolerable levels of anxiety as she faces the prospect of going through adolescence. The unconscious part of the anorectic's personality defends her from overwhelming levels of anxiety. The anorectic's unconscious operates outside of her awareness and shifts the focus of her internal developmental fears externally upon food and the fear of obesity. Once her unconscious takes control, the anorectic no longer has free choice over her behavior.

The symptoms of anorexia nervosa can be regarded as communication through gestures. Food and the fear of obesity serve as symbols. The anorectic experiences high levels of anxiety when she eats as this logically, leads to weight gain and adult physical maturity. Her fear of obesity, therefore, compels her to exercise, to vomit, or to purge in order to remove the food she has eaten and to retain her childhood dependency status. By controlling her weight, she also controls her anxiety. Losing weight is associated with anxiety reduction and, therefore, her symptomatic behavior becomes reinforced and habitual.

Anorexia nervosa, like all other mental illnesses, is destined to fail as a solution to problems. The struggle over the anorectic's life problems is fought in the wrong arena: food. Her symptoms dominate more and more of her everyday functioning. She moves further and further away from reality. Symptoms serve a protective function for the anorectic. They help her control her anxiety. Without these symptoms, her anxiety might reach panic proportions. The unconscious, through the formation of her symptoms, has shifted the battle for autonomy away from normal adolescent issues onto her concern for controlling her weight and food intake. She is no longer solving problems directed toward adult maturity.

Symptoms are only surface pictures of the anorectic's behavior. One symptom may hold a variety of meanings and satisfy a variety of needs for a specific anorectic. These meanings can only be discovered through the process of individual therapy. There are, however, some general psychological interpretations applied to the meaning of the anorectic's symptoms. These psychological interpretations suggest that the anorectic's symptoms are related to her low self-esteem, and to conflicts associated with the issue of autonomy; and to the issue of establishing a female sexual identity.

LOW SELF-ESTEEM

The symptoms of anorexia nervosa originate to protect her fragile self-esteem. The anorectic is unable to face developmental tasks which many adolescents take casually. Anorexia nervosa serves a protective function by providing the anorectic with an alternative way to experience success and to elevate her self-esteem. The anorectic is extremely proud of her ability to lose weight and control the shape of her body. Her success at weight control compensates for her feelings of inadequacy and insignificance. She feels and looks "special." The power which the anorectic has over others in her family is a secondary gain of the illness. Through her starvation, she realizes that she controls the behavior of her parents and siblings. She has turned the tables on them. Instead of feeling like a helpless puppet reacting to the control of her parents, she now pulls their strings. The anorectic's withdrawal from others also serves to protect her self-esteem. She avoids unpleasant discussions concerning her eating behaviors. She withdraws not only from others but from all interests except food. She eventually spends more and more time alone, and retreats further into the mental illness.

AUTONOMY

The onset of anorexia nervosa has been associated with situations involving separations, such as; going away to school, a sibling leaving home, marrying, or a loss through death. Many anorectics are unable to cope with separation from the family although they will try to be independent by going away to school. Anorectics actually prefer to remain at home, and many do not return to their college or university. The anorectic is unable to become autonomous and mature as a result of her family situation and her own overpowering dependency needs. Unconsciously, the anorectic wishes to maintain a dependent position within the family. The anorectic comes from an excessively close family. Her parents are overprotective and controlling, and she is never allowed the opportunity to develop autonomy. A mutual dependency between the anorectic and her parents blocks any movement toward independence and separation. The psychological task of disengaging from her parents is particularly frightening for the anorectic.

Mother/Child Relationship

The literature focuses on the quality of the anorectic's relationship to her mother as central to the anorectics psychological conflict. Many anorectics report a childhood controlled by their mothers. They feel considerable anger and hostility toward their mothers and also resent their dependence on their mothers. The anorectic's relationship with her mother is extremely ambivalent. On the one hand she wants to be independent of her mother and at the same time, she wants to remain dependent of her mother.

The anorectic's mother is often afraid of her daughter's striving for independence. In these situations mothers do not impart an attitude of confidence which is necessary for the anorectic to take the risks associated with separation. Another problem associated with the mother's relationship with the anorectic is the mother's lack of encouragement of her daughter's self-directed behavior. The current lack of initiative in the anorectic is attributed to the absence of a consistent response of the mother to any of her daughter's self-initiated behavior when the anorectic was a young child.[32] Some clinicians interpret the symbolic meaning of the anorectic's refusal to eat as representing a rejection of her mother. Mothers are normally associated with food, and cooking, and they are responsible for feeding their children.

One purpose of the anorectic's symptoms is to help her avoid confronting the psychological task of separating from her parents. She still experiences, however, a strong drive toward independence. She fights the battle of independence from her parents over the issue of food. The anorectic achieves absolute control over her body. Through her severe dieting she also becomes independent from the sensations of hunger and fatigue, and even from food, a basic necessity of life. Much of the anorectic's overt behavior gives the appearance of being independent. As the disorder progresses, she becomes thinner and more dependent.

SEXUALITY

At adolescence the anorectic experiences new sexual tensions and impulses which are associated with the emergence of puberty and an increase in the production of sexual hormones. The anorectic also must integrate these sexual feelings with her body changes and her new secondary sex characteristics. Ultimately, the anorectic must establish an adult female sexual identity. The anorectic's family's sexual values and current social conditions make her fearful of confronting the issues associated with an adult female sexual identity. The psychological process involved in establishing a female identity is extremely complex and begins from the moment of birth. In the current society, this difficult developmental task becomes even more complicated and creates additional psychological stress. Over the last two decades, there have been considerable changes in the role of the female in society. Women are now choosing between motherhood, professional careers, or the superwoman role, which combines both motherhood and a career.

The anorectic's family attitude toward sexual matters is extremely conservative and can even be characterized as repressive. The emergence of their adolescent daughter's sexuality is threatening to her parents as it re-surfaces their own sexual difficulties. There is a distinct attitude within the family that sex is taboo. The anorectic is fearful of her sexual urges and their implications for heterosexual intimacy. Some anorectics report their symptoms started following a sexually stressful experience or associated with their menstruation. The onset of the disorder may be associated with sexual relations in the marriage or the birth of a child.

Menstruation is often an abrupt and startling event for adolescent girls. Many anorectics begin puberty at an early age and are overwhelmed by their rapid sexual development. They experience their bodily changes and an increase in instinctual energy as shocking and tragic. Menstruation is a definite physiological statement of her womanhood. Through the cessation of menstruation, the anorexic unconsciously denies her femininity. Amenorrhea is a somatic expression of her sexual conflict and symbolically represents an infantile regression to the prepubertal stages of development. Many anorectics are unconcerned about the cessation of their menstruation or are actually pleased when their periods stop. The emergence of the adolescent's secondary sex characteristics, coupled with the implication these experiences hold for heterosexual intimacy, is particularly frightening to the anorectic. Symptoms form to protect her from facing these frightening sexual issues. Her dieting behavior and her goal of being thin serve as a camouflage for her sexual conflicts.

BODY LANGUAGE AND DISTORTION

As a youngster progresses toward adulthood, verbal skills become the major source of intrapersonal and interpersonal communication. When the adolescent ego is overwhelmed with anxiety, the individual regresses to an earlier form of communication "action" language. Drives and conflicts are somatized and the individual resorts to "body" language as a form of symbolic communication.[33] This regression to "body" language is clearly present in the symptoms of anorexia nervosa. The young girl distorts her body image through extreme loss of weight, and also psychogenically stops her menstruation through amenorrhea. These symptoms express a desperate attempt on the anorexic's part to halt her sexual development. Anna Freud stated that children with rigid and immature egos do not accommodate to new mature forms of sexuality, instead the ego inhibits and distorts their sexual maturity.[34]

Psychologically, the anorectic's body represents the degree of acceptance or rejection of her female sexual identification. The most characteristic feature of the anorectic is the grotesque distortion and emaciation of her body. By starving it, her way of neutering the body, she is making it less obviously feminine. This emaciation leads to a total renunciation of sexuality: sexual impulses are eliminated from consciousness.

A Child Again

Weight loss combined with amenorrhea changes her appearance to a prepubertal child; breasts diminished greatly, and she regards herself as a child. She does not have the body form of a sexually mature adult woman. This frees her of her sexuality and the burden of guilt and anxiety associated with it. The anorectic considers herself to be her parent's delightful little girl. She diets away her sexual characteristics and returns to the comfort and safety of the childhood state. The disorder successfully reverses the normal process of physical maturity.

A Body Image Delusion

Even though the anorectic's physical body size is small and thin as a child's, she still considers herself to be overweight. The anorectic's overestimation of her body size forces her to continue her starvation. Her insistence that she is too fat despite her emaciation represents delusional thinking. The anorectic distorts external reality and holds on to her false belief despite any evidence to the contrary. She cannot see the dangers inherent in her behavior, and continues her destructive dieting behavior with determination. The anorectic does not, however, distort the body size of other anorectics. She can perceive others as too thin, but she will assert that she is not as thin as they are when, in fact, she is far more emaciated than the other anorectics.[35]

This symptom bolsters the other symptoms and keeps the illness self-perpetuating. The distortion of body image keeps her in her childlike body appearance and protects her from any awareness of her sexuality. She holds stubbornly to her belief that she looks good with her current weight and that she will look even better if she loses more weight. She has an attitude of unconcern toward her skeletal appearance: "la belle indifference." She lives in a whole world of denial and states that there is nothing either physically or emotionally wrong with her.

FAMILY DECISION

The anorectic's parents wonder what they have done wrong in bringing up this child as they have had only her best interests at heart. They start criticizing each other for past transgressions which they believe could have been responsible. They suffer from guilt and this limits their ability to objectively judge the seriousness of their daughter's psychological condition. Out of desperation the parents take their emaciated daughter to a physician. When the physician does not find a medical explanation, they take her to another physician. The anorectic will visit a string of doctors; pediatrician, internist, and gynecologist. She may admit to the physician some abdominal pain, difficulty in sleeping, or loss of appetite, but otherwise insist that nothing is wrong. Ironically, any suggestion of a psychological problem is quickly discounted by the anorectic and her parents.

The severe weight loss is observable in her physical appearance. She looks pale and gaunt; her legs and arms are visibly skinny, and her eyes are sunken. Her appearance approaches skeletal proportions as every vein in her body is visible. The anorectic's dieting and food obsession take her deeper into the world of mental illness and further from reality. She has destroyed her normal eating habits. Next, she may destroy herself.

There comes a point when the parents can no longer endure the agony of watching their daughter waste away and refuse their help. The illness brings misery to family members who suffer along with the anorectic. They feel helpless and frustrated with their daughter's inability to recognize her emaciation and the danger of her situation. They take her to the hospital hoping that she will have the benefit of highly technical laboratory tests, and that an organic basis will be found for her condition. As they enter the hospital, the anguish of the parents' ordeal is visible in their faces and their posture. Hospital staff members speculate with confidence that the young girl is most likely another victim of anorexia nervosa. Two decades ago, only a few girls with anorexia nervosa walked through those hospital doors. Now, it is a regular occurrence.

Chapter 4

AT THE HOSPITAL

THE ANORECTIC is taken to the hospital by her parents against her will. She is usually brought during the advanced stages of the illness. Her parents were unable to recognize that she had a psychological problem, nor does the anorectic realize that she has a psychological disturbance. Parents report that they thought their daughter was only going through an adolescent phase. They felt they could handle the problem themselves. Now they see her emaciation and they no longer believe her behavior is typical of an adolescent stage. They bring her to the hospital and plead with the physicians to save their daughter's life.

The anorectic's self-esteem is maintained by the collective efforts of her pathological symptoms. Without them, she could experience a level of anxiety approaching panic proportions. She is emotionally as fragile as her fragile physical appearance. When the anorectic is brought to the hospital by her parents, she is proud of her lean appearance. She truly does not understand why everyone is worried about her weight. The anorectic is also terrified of the hospital. She believes that the hospital staff is going to force her to eat and rob her of her "specialness."

The anorectic's physical appearance creates emotional turmoil in those who observe her. People in an affluent society are not used to seeing victims of starvation. The anorectic's cheeks are sunken. She is skin and bones, and her veins are visible through her dry skin. Her eyes are glazed and lack luster. Her expression is doleful, however, she is still reserved and mistrustful. The anorectic does not gesture much nor change her facial expression. She is tense and frozen in her appearance. Her face resembles that of an old woman, yet her body resembles that of a child's.

The anorectic may be wearing layers of clothing, long sleeved blouses or cardigans to keep herself warm. She may volunteer that she always feels cold; that no matter what she wears she cannot feel warmth.

She may admit to not sleeping well and having a few stomach pains. She will insist, however, she does not need a doctor, nor does she need to be in the hospital. She may also reluctantly admit that she thinks of food a lot and, therefore, has some difficulty concentrating. She will not volunteer, however, her terrifying fear of becoming fat or her vomiting and laxative abuse. The anorectic rejects any implication that she is ill. If anyone makes a statement suggesting that she is starving to death, she registers disbelief. She maintains that she is healthy and that there is nothing wrong with her. No amount of conversation will change her opinion. She will not agree to hospitalization.

MEDICAL EXAMINATION

The physician's first priority is an evaluation of the nutritional status of the patient. If she appears to be in a crisis situation, then immediate medical treatment is initiated to insure survival. After an evaluation of her nutritional status, the physician will search for an organic explanation for her symptoms.

During the advanced stages of anorexia nervosa the anorectic will state that she has lost her appetite. This could be the result of a number of medical conditions. The physician performs a series of diagnostic investigations to determine if there is an organic explanation for her emaciation. Some physical conditions which may be responsible for weight loss include: structural disorders of the digestive system (esophogeal stenosis), Simmond's disease (a pituitary gland defect), juvenile diabetes, parasitic infection, Chron's disease (regional enteritis), and malignancy. Anorectics, however, desire their weight loss and do not register any concern about their physical condition.

The physician conducts a physical examination to seek a medical explanation for her condition. The most obvious finding of the physical examination is her substantial weight loss. Other findings which are secondary to her malnutrition include: dry, flaky skin; constipation, lanugo (fine, downy hairs), weak and brittle nails, bradycardia (persistent resting pulse of sixty or less), amenorrhea, head hair loss, edema, cyanotic extremeties (icy feet and hands), hypotension (low blood pressure), low body temperature, and possibly epileptic seizures. Some findings from the laboratory examination include: hypoglycemia, low thyroid hormone, low production of sex hormones (leutenizing hormone, estrogen) and a reduced basal metabolic rate. The findings from the physical examination and laboratory tests suggest that the girl is suffering from the effects of starvation.

A Starved Body

Towards the end stages, the anorectic has eaten practically nothing. In addition, her habits of vomiting, purging and exercising have removed food from her body before the digestive tract could extract necessary nutrients. Anorectics may lose as much as 25-50% of their body weight over a period just a few months. During starvation, the body is forced to break down its own muscle tissue to obtain essential proteins. If the starvation progresses further, the anorectic would be in a medical crisis of life-threatening proportions. The body tries to protect the anorectic from any further loss of protein by lowering the metabolic rate. This process helps the body to conserve energy and, therefore, prevent additional weight loss.

The lowering of the metabolic weight works in direct opposition to the anorectic's desire to lose weight. As a result of the body's adaptations, if the anorectic eats just a little more than ususal, she will add weight quickly because the lower metabolic rate will still be operating. The body is primed to gain weight easily with less food than previously. She, therefore, must lower her caloric intake further to compensate for the lower basal metabolic rate.

Another adaptive measure associated with altering of the metabolic rate is the conservation of energy through lowering the body temperature. In addition, the blood volume decreases which results in a slower heart beat, and reduced blood pressure. If the caloric restriction is severe enough, poor circulation and low body temperature leave the anorectic feeling very cold.

For the anorectic who resorts to vomiting, the loss of nutrients and potassium is greatly facilitated. Because food is vomited before it leaves the stomach, essential amino acids are lost. Potassium, a critical body electrolyte, is highly concentrated in stomach acids and it is, therefore, lost. The use of diuretics will increase the excretion of fluid which leads to dehydration and further loss of potassium. The consequences of the anorectic's vomiting and laxative abuse in addition to the food restriction, create a dangerous electrolyte imbalance within her body. Potassium is essential to many life processes: it regulates heart rhythm and at low levels it can lead to death from cardiac and kidney failure.

Many anorectics limit their liquid intake as well as their food intake. This can lead to a dangerous level of dehydration. The use of diuretics adds additional complications to the body's water regulation system. Periods of edema are experienced with swollen ankles and feet alternating with periods of dehydration. In addition, anorectics complain of early satiety, epigastric discomfort and spontaneous vomiting. There are medical reports which describe impaired gastric emptying and abnormal gastric mobility occurring in anorectics.[36]

AMENORRHEA

The hypothalamus plays a major role in the release of hormones which are responsible for menstruation. Many physicians believe that a dysfunction of the hypothalamus accounts for the anorectic's symptom of amenorrhea. Laboratory results indicate that the anorectic has low excretion rates of the sexual hormones, leutenizing hormone, and estrogen, which are responsible for ovulation. The anorectic's sex hormonal secretion pattern returns to a pre-pubertal level found in children.[37] There is general agreement among clinicians that the hypothalamus must be involved in anorexia nervosa for amenorrhea to occur.

Critical Weight Hypothesis

There is, however, another medical hypothesis offered to explain the cessation of the anorectic's menstruation. While the hypothalamus is necessarily involved since it controls the production of sex hormones, the critical weight theory suggests that the hypothalamus dysfunction and amenorrhea are related to the anorectic's weight loss and nutritional deficiencies associated with the dieting. The critical weight theory states that amenorrhea will occur in all women, pubertal and post-pubertal, when the percentage of body fat falls below 17%.[38]

The critical weight theory claims that puberty, as indicated by menses, occurs at the weight of 47.8 +/-4.6 kg. (110 plus/minus 10.58 pounds) with a corresponding fat percent threshold regardless of a woman's height or age.[39] According to the critical weight theory the anorectic's weight loss possibly initiates a reaction in the hypothalamus which results in a reduced production of the sexual hormones.

Opponents of the critical weight theory acknowledge that many individuals do stop menstruating as a result of starvation. They do not, however, believe that this totally explains the onset of amenorrhea in anorectics. Some anorectics report the cessation of their periods before any weight loss has occurred. As many as 20% to 65% of women who develop anorexia nervosa ceased menstruating before any weight loss or dieting behavior.[40]

STARVATION RESEARCH

Many of the symptoms of anorexia nervosa have been associated with the general effects of starvation. The anorectic's medical complications are similar to victims of starvation, such as; constipation, amenorrhea, low pressure and low body temperature. One research study, Minnesota Experiment on Starvation, investigated the effects of eating only one-half the caloric intake on thirty-six World War II conscientious objectors who volunteered to participate in this project for six months. Some of the results of this study correspond to the behavior observed in anorectics, such as; poor concentration, depression, irritability, dizzy spells, loss of hunger and strength. Like anorectics, starvation victims demonstrated bizarre food tastes and preferences. They would daydream and read about food. Food was a major topic of their conversation.[41]

HYPOTHALAMUS

The results of the physical examination and laboratory tests of the anorectic indicate that she has observable medical problems. Medical research into anorexia nervosa is trying to determine whether the anorectic's physical problems are caused by an organic dysfunction or are a result of her malnutrition. The organ most likely involved in anorexia nervosa is the hypothalamus which is an area of the brain connected to the pituitary. The hypothalamus controls many diverse functions, some of which are related to the anorectic's physical problems. The hypothalamus regulates menstruation through the production of sex hormones. It also regulates appetite, sleep, body temperature, body fluids and metabolism.

Eating is initiated by activity of the lateral hypothalamus, the feeding center, and it is inhibited by the activity of the ventromedial hypothalamus, the satiety center. Destruction of the lateral hypothalamus produces aphagia; a total lack of eating. Destruction of the ventromedial hypothalamus produces hyperphagia, excessive eating. These parallel the clinical features of anorexia nervosa where the anorectic alternates from lack of eating to binge behavior.[42] Research experiments on animals indicate that lesions on the hypothalamus can lead to animals demonstrating an aversion to food and/or lack of appetite, or to excessive and uncontrollable eating which leads to obesity. In the literature there are reports of women who exhibit symptoms similar to anorexia nevosa and have tumors of the hypothalamus.[43]

Critics of the hypothalamus theory point out that many of the anorectic's medical abnormalities are reversible with the normalization of her weight. This raises the question of the existence of any permanent hypothalamic dysfunction. While hypothalamic tumors in women have been proposed as an explanation of the anorectic's symptoms, the general view is that a majority of hypothalamus tumors do not produce symptoms associated with anorexia nervosa. Pathological tumors of the hypothalamus are seldom mentioned in the post mortem reports of anorectics.[44]

The controvesy over mind and body dualism still exists today with regard to the cause of anorexia nervosa. While it is apparent that there are hormonal and physical complications associated with anorexia nervosa, many experts believe that the the origin of anorexia nervosa is psychological. Medical research has not as yet revealed any conclusive evidence that the symptoms of anorexia nervosa are caused by a primary hypothalamus dysfunction.

PSYCHOLOGICAL EXAMINATION

The psychologist assesses the anorectic's mental status through clinical interviews and through the use of psychological tests. Depending upon the severity of her malnutrition, the anorectic can experience psychological problems associated with her starvation. Some of the psychological effects of starvation include: loss of concentration, mental confusion, depression, and irritability. The psychologist may need to wait until the anorectic's physical condition improves before conducting the psychological examination.

Differential Diagnosis

The patient's physical appearance suggests that she may have anorexia nervosa. She states that she has lost her appetite and that she has no desire for food. Other mental illnesses include these same complaints and also lead to self starvation. Schizophrenia is a form of mental illness which includes bizarre eating behavior. A paranoid schizophrenic may refuse to eat and, consequently, lose a considerable amount of weight. Unlike the anorectic, however, the paranoid schizophrenic gives as a motive for refusing to eat the excuse that food is poisoned or contaminated. Dysphagia, a fear of swallowing, is another mental illness which can be easily distinguished from anorexia nervosa. The anorectic, however, does not report a fear of swallowing. Other mental illnesses, depression and hysterical neurosis, include the symptom of a loss of appetite.

Depression

The onset of anorexia nervosa has been associated with such events such as leaving home, or after a humiliating remark about her physical appearance. These experiences suggest an episode of depression. The anorectic's physical behavior, however, differs considerably from those individuals diagnosed as depressives. The depressed individual would not be hyperactive, but would demonstrate slow lethargic movements. The depressive also would not demonstrate any pride in being thin. On the contrary, a characteristic feature of depression is a dysphoric mood with a picture of misery and constant accusations of self blame. The depressive would complain and be additionally distressed by the severe weight loss. Conversely, the anorectic is only unhappy when she gains weight. She will still express enjoyment on losing weight and state that the refusal of food is a pleasurable experience. An individual who is depressed experiences a general impairment of all functioning and often cannot cope enough to work. The anorectic still manages somehow to cope with work despite her physical and emotional problems. Anorectics do experience depression particularly after any binge eating behavior. Results on the Minnesota Multiphase Personality Test psychological instrument show that anorectic's tend to have high scores on the scale which measure depression.[45] In many cases, therefore, depression and anorexia nervosa may co-exist.

Hysterical Neurosis

Individuals who suffer from hysterical neurosis complain of somatic distress, abdominal and gastric pains, in the absence of any organic pathology. Their complaints can lead to feeding difficulties and emaciation in order to avoid psychological distress. The hysteric is motivated by the secondary gains of her behavior. She uses her symptoms too obtain control over her environment and to escape from an intolerable personal situation. The hysteric tries to elicit sympathy from others and proclaims her inability to eat. She demonstrates, "la belle indifference" to her physical disability regardless of how serious the condition appears to be. She will express confidence and optimism that her condition will be cured.

Similar to the hysteric, the anorectic experiences a secondary gain associated with her illness which is the control over her environment and the manipulation of others to protect her low self-esteem. The anorectic also demonstrates "la belle indifference" toward her emaciation and the seriousness of her physical condition. Unlike the hysteric, however, the anorectic does not believe that she has any physical condition that needs a medical cure. The anorectic neither hides the fact that she does not eat nor does she seek sympathy. She also does not use her illness to avoid responsibilities. She will struggle, despite tiredness and weakness, and continue working.

The psychologist, therefore, rules out other mental illnesses, such as paranoid schizophrenia, depression and hysteria. Next, the psychologist must diagnose which specific eating disorder the patient may have: bulimia or anorexia nervosa. The victims of these two eating disorders share similar characteristics. They all perceive themselves as too fat. This differentiation will be critical to the implementation of an appropriate treatment plan.

Bulimia

Bulimia is an eating disorder which includes the symptoms of binging on large quantities of food, as much as 8,000 calories, within a short time. Bulimics resort to self-induced vomiting, diuretics and laxative abuse to avoid any weight gain. She differs from the anorectic in that she is more conscious of the inappropriateness of her behavior. She suffers tremendous depression and self-deprecation over her binging, vomiting, and purging behavior. The bulimic may always remain at near normal or normal weight. Since she consumes thousands of calories, some are digested and she, therefore, does not reach the low weights of the anorectic. Bulimics usually do not demonstrate amenorrhea; conversely, the anorectic ceases to menstruate.

Anorexia Nervosa

Anorectics differ with regard to their weight control methods. Some anorectics rely exclusively upon food restriction and excessive exercising as weight control methods. They are clinically referred to as "dieters" or "restrictors." Anorectics who additionally engage in binging, vomiting, and purging behavior are referred to as "vomiters" or "bulimarexics." This differentiation will be critical to the implementation of an appropriate treatment plan.

All anorectics begin by relying only on dieting and exercising techniques: the bulimarexics develop the binge/vomit/purge pattern. The bulimarexic does not have the self-discipline necessary to stay on her food restrictive diet. Between periods of starvation, she will overeat or binge, and then resort to vomiting or purging. These behaviors are similar to the symptoms of bulimia. The bulimarexic experiences serious medical complications associated with her vomiting and purging behavior.

DIAGNOSIS

A team of specialists, physician, psychologist, nutritionist, social worker and nurse, confers to discuss the findings from the patient's physical and psychological examinations. The physician reports the results of the girl's physical examination and laboratory tests. The physician's conclusion is that she suffers from the generalized effects of starvation and not from any specific medical illness. The psychologist reports the girl's symptoms are consistent with a diagnosis of anorexia nervosa, a psychological disturbance. The hospital team designs a treatment plan which consists of feeding techniques to improve her nutritional health and psychotherapy techniques to improve her emotional health.

Admission

When the anorectic is in a state of medical emergency, there is unanimous agreement that she must be admitted to the hospital and that her nutritional needs must be given priority treatment. The decision for medical treatment depends upon the severity of her weight loss. Admission is related not only to the level of her emaciation, but on the status of her metabolic complications and electrolyte disturbance which have caused death in some anorectics.[32] If the anorectic is severely malnour-ished, hospitalization has the advantage of providing control over her eating environment. Hospital admission would also be warranted if the anorectic's behavior suggests a high risk of suicide.

When the anorectic is not in a state of medical emergency, clinicians differ with regard to the necessity of hospitalization. Some clinicians favor treating the anorectic and her family on an outpatient basis and only admit her if she fails to respond to treatment. Many professionals, however, maintain that the anorectic is best treated in a hospital milieu setting. In the hospital, the anorectic will benefit from the services of a team of professionals. Her weight will be monitored around the clock and her food intake closely supervised. She will receive intense individ-ual psychotherapy to help her with her emotional problems as she gains weight. Additionally, the family will receive on-going family therapy ses-sions. Hospitals specializing in eating disorders offer the most compre-hensive treatment program available for anorexia nervosa.

PARENT CONFERENCE

The findings from the physical examination and laboratory tests in-dicate that the anorectic suffers from the generalized effects of starvation and not from any specific mental illness. The physician reports to the parents that their daughter's symptoms are the result of a psychological disturbance and/or impaired family relationships. The physician recom-mends that their daughter be admitted to the hospital. The hospital staff will immediately begin to treat her for nutritional needs and implement a feeding program to increase her weight. She will receive individual psychological therapy. The family will be expected to attend family therapy.

The physician strongly indicates that improving their daughter's nu-tritional state does not cure her. The cure must be accomplished through psychological therapy. Their daughter needs to understand why she de-veloped anorexia nervosa to deal with the problems of her life. The phy-sician also informs the parents that the family needs to make changes along with the anorectic.

Parents of anorectics demonstrate different reactions upon admitting their daughter to the hospital for medical and psychiatric care. Some parents maintain the belief that their daughter is not really mentally ill. A few parents are hopeful and react with a sense of gratification. The majority of parents are bewildered by the thought of their daughter being mentally ill. She was always a normal happy girl who did not display an indication of emotional problems. After the initial shock, the anorectic's parents tend to feel guilty. They torture themselves with doubts about their own parenting behavior and search for things they did that could have caused their daughter's mental illness. They believe that through their own, faults and ignorance, they have damaged their child.

ANORECTIC'S REACTION

Disbelief! She is not starving to death. She is healthy and feels fine. She resists the decision to hospitalize her. She is steadfast that she will not eat, and she is reluctant to accept treatment. She will plead, cry, and beg her parents not to put her in the hospital. She threatens them with all sorts of terrible accusations, questions their love, and begs them not to leave her. The anorectic is told that she needs to be in the hospital because she has damaged herself physically with her starvation. She is reassured that the hospital will care for her nutritional needs and increase her weight. At the same time they understand her fears, and assure her that the treatment will not make her fat.

The anorectic has arrived at the point where her internal physical needs and external environmental pressures force her to do what she has struggled for so long not to do: eat. She now experiences fear associated with the loss of control over her food intake. She must get out of the hospital. The anorectic vacillates emotionally between anger and depression. She states emphatically that there is nothing wrong with her and she wants to go home. She is scared, and even distrusts her parents. She makes their life extremely difficult for them during every visit. The anorectic promises that she will eat if her parents will take her out of the hospital. Sometimes the anorectic succeeds, and her parents sign her out of the hospital against medical advice. If she is old enough, she may even discharge herself from accepting treatment.

LEGAL CONSIDERATIONS

Anorexia nervosa is life threatening, however, the anorectic is not aware of her physical danger. She is afraid to return to normal weight, therefore, she refuses in-patient treatment. For the small percentage of

anorectics whose life and health are in danger, legal commitment is justi-
fied as a last resort.[46] The patient must be informed of all aspects of this
decision. She must be reassured that what is being done is to prevent her
possible death or irreversible body damage. The result of this decision
has enormous psychological consequences, especially regarding control
over her body and this issue must be addressed during psychotherapy.

Chapter 5

TECHNIQUES FOR WEIGHT GAIN

TREATMENT OF THE anorectic focuses upon two aspects. One aspect is symptom oriented and concentrates on weight restoration and normalization of eating behavior. The second aspect of treatment is problem oriented and focuses on the anorectic's underlying emotional conflicts. There are several treatment techniques used with the anorectic in order to address all the aspects of the illness. Treatment programs consider the interrelationship of all factors operating in the disorder and, therefore, include a combination of treatment procedures. The short term goal of treatment is to remove the patient from physical danger and to focus on weight gain. Treatment programs include special diets, behavioral therapy, oral and tube feedings. The long term goal of treatment focuses on the psychological aspects of the disorder and on the maintenance of normal weight. Treatment programs include individual, family, art, and group therapy.

Psychotherapy must be started either simultaneously or after enough weight gain to insure her active participation in the process. Some anorectics suffer from the psychological effects of starvation; loss of concentration, mental confusion and irritability. Therefore, they do not have the capability to benefit from psychotherapy. The psychologist's role in the beginning may be just to inform her that her life is in danger and that the hospital staff will begin a program to increase her weight. The psychologist reassures her that the hospital staff will not let her become fat.

Initial treatment is often aimed at the normalization of the anorectic's weight which is generally the average weight for her age, sex and height. This would appear to be a simple task. All that is necessary is to increase her food intake and to decrease her hyperactivity. The major problem is to persuade her to cooperate with something she is determined not to do.

Consequently, treatment is plagued with problems and difficulties. How much can the anorectic be helped when she does not admit that she needs help? She is being treated against her will.

FEEDING METHODS

The approach used to increase anorectic's weight follows a careful evaluation of her medical test results. The medical care of her undernutrition and electrolyte disturbance differs according to the stage of weight loss. Specific types of medical complications and the amount of weight loss determine the treatment approach. If the anorectic is just below nutritional need, the treatment approach may be gradual oral feeding. If she has a more serious nutritional deficiency, treatment is more difficult as complications can occur during refeeding. Finally, if she is severely emaciated, she may be in a state of nutritional crisis, and death may occur.

The first objective of treatment is her renourishment. The medical problem is to determine how this can best be accomplished. Physicians need to balance the potential benefits of a particular approach against the risks of using that method. Treatment for re-feeding can be achieved by oral feeding with high caloric supplements and bed rest, or by forced feeding using nasogastric or gastrostomy tubes, or parentally.

Tube feeding methods are used only as a last resort when it is essential to overcome the potentially dangerous loss of weight. Under these conditions, the anorectic's metabolic status needs immediate attention. The anorectic is either too weak to eat orally or is resistant to oral methods. Nonetheless, she is in urgent need of nutrition, and, therefore, forced feeding methods will be used to achieve weight gain. Forced feeding procedures may require the physical restraint of anorectics who are uncooperative. There are certain risks such as gastric infarction and rupture, and vomiting with aspiration, associated with tube feeding procedures.

Total Parenteral Nutrition is another forced feeding method used for patients typically near death. It is a powerful tool under these conditions. The procedure requires that a nutritional solution is given via catheter placed in sub-clavian vein in chest. Through this intravenous method, the physician can supplement high powered nutrients and the patient will gain weight rapidly. There are specific complications associated with total parenteral feeding such as malposition of the catheter placement leading to pneumothorax and hemothorax infection at the catheter site leading to sepsis and venus thrombosis.[48] There are teams which specialize in total parental feeding and this reduces the incidence of complications. However, the risk of death as a result of the procedure still remains significant.[48]

✓Although forced feeding techniques yield good short term results in the form of weight gain, there are considerable physiological and psychological risks associated with forced feeding techniques. The anorectic is against any procedure which leads to weight gain. Forced feeding procedures completely overpowers the anoretic. She considers them to be coercive and painful techniques.

As a consequence of their starvation, anorectics can have very low levels of potassium. Some are given medication or oral potassium to correct this situation. Others may receive potassium through intravenous fluids used to supplement their nutrition. The anorectic's potassium level needs to be monitored continuously as she may resort to vomiting surreptiously during the treatment.

Bed rest is often prescribed along with a tranquilizer to decrease her energy. A major tranquilizer, bed rest and a high calorie diet have been reported to facilitate weight gain.[49] Under this regimen, the anorectic has decreased caloric expenditure and decreased resistance to eating as a result of the tranquilizer. Some weight gain can be attributed to side effects of the medication. Long term effects of tranquilizers are disappointing. While the anorectic may gain weight easily, once the tranquilizer is discontinued, the anorectic returns to her low weight. Many anorectics also have symptoms of depression. Anti-depressants are administered to alleviate the symptoms of depression, not to treat the anorexia nervosa. Electro-convulsive shock treatment has also been reported to relieve depression in some anorectics.[16]

BEHAVIOR THERAPY

Clinicians prefer to use oral feeding techniques to increase the anorectic's weight rather than forced tube feedings. Behavior therapy is an alternative psychological treatment which has been successfully used to achieve short term, rapid weight gain.[50] Behavior techniques avoid the negative side affects of drugs and tube feedings while still facilitating the anorectic's weight gain.

Behavior therapy is based on the assumption that all behavior is learned. According to behavior therapy, the symptoms of anorexia nervosa are maladaptive learned patterns of behavior. A behavior is learned whenever it is repeatedly followed by reinforcement from the environment. For example, the anorectic's food refusal is reinforced by the attention she receives from her family. Her desire to be thin is reinforced by the social approval she receives from others who compliment her slim appearance.

A behavior therapy program attempts to correct the anorectic's maladaptive behavior by manipulating various types of reinforcements. The behavior therapy program is based on the principle that behavior can be changed by frequently pairing a particular type of reinforcement with a specific behavior. The application of the reinforcement follows the performance of the behavior and this reinforcement process increases the likelihood that the desired behavior will occur again. Behavior therapy programs consist of the application of positive reinforcement, negative reinforcement, and punishment.

In a positive reinforcement program, the therapist attempts to restore the anorectic's normal patterns of eating by manipulating various kinds of positive reinforcers, objects, or events which serve as rewards. The anorectic receives a reward whenever she demonstrates the desired behavior of the treatment program. The assumption is that the anorectic's behavior will change as a result of pairing the reward with the desired behavior. Behavior programs may differ with regard to which specific anorectic behavior will be selected for positive reinforcement. The anorectic may receive reinforcement for a specific amount of weight gain; for certain types of eating behavior, counting mouthfuls; or for completing her meal within a limited time period.

There are also a variety of different types of rewards given to the anorectic. She may receive privileges such as visits from her parents, visits home on a pass, access to the game room, and other activities which the anorectic finds rewarding. One study used the anorectic's desire for physical activity as a reward. This study investigated the amount of activity anorectics engaged in while in the hospital. Clinicians placed pedometers on anorectic patients and found that during a free access period, anorectics walked on the average of 6.8 miles per day in addition to repetitive climbing up a flight of stairs. This contrasts with the results obtained from women of normal weight whose average daily activity consisted of 4.9 miles per day. Therapists designed a successful treatment program which rewarded the anorectic for weight gain by increasing her access to engage in physical activity.[51]

In a negative reinforcement program, an aversive condition which the anorectic finds intolerable is removed whenever the anorectic achieves the desired behavior. One study found that anorectics gained weight in order to reduce the dosage of the tranquilizer which was prescribed. Anorectics strongly dislike bed rest and the sedating side effects of the medication. The clinicians linked the reduction in medication to the anorectic's weight gain, and this program successfully stimulated weight gain.[51] Punishment is also used in some behavior treatment plans. If the anorectic does not achieve the desired behavior, she would incur some negative consequences such as; isolation, forced bed rest, and forced feeding. She resents the coercive nature of the punishment and is likely to retain a negative attitude toward the hospital as a result of this form of manipulative treatment.

Behavior therapists design behavior therapy programs based on the principles of positive reinforcement in order to increase the anorectic's weight. The clinician specifies the weight gain necessary for the anorectic to receive a reward. The anorectic constructs a list of rewards that will be used when she achieves the desired weight gain. A behavior program could also include negative consequences. For example, if the anorectic loses any weight during the program, she may be isolated on the ward or tube fed until the weight gain is achieved. The clinician and anorectic draw up a contract specifying the conditions of the behavior program. The clinician carefully explains the conditions of the program to the anorectic. She must clearly understand that she will receive specific privileges or rewards contingent upon her achieving the desired weight. Programs are designed to reward the anorectic for small amounts of continuous weight gain. She will be considered for hospital discharge when she ultimately achieves a normal body weight for her age and height along with the improvement in her psychological status. Anorectics are shocked by the weight criterion set for discharge. They are constantly trying to make deals connecting their discharge to a much lower weight level.

Hospital Team

There are many specialists who work with the anorectic during her hospital stay: occupational therapist, physical therapist, dietician, and nurses. Each specialist has a specific responsibility regarding the anorectic's treatment. They are informed concerning her specific treatment program and assist in assessing whether the anorectic has met the criterion of desired behavior and, therefore, whether she should receive the reward. Generally, the anorectic receives attention from the hospital staff when she demonstrates the desired behavior, and they withdraw their attention when she does not demonstrate the behavior. She is not coerced or made to participate in the program. The anorectic chooses either to gain weight and receive a reward, or to lose weight and not receive anything.

Dietician

Anorectic patients generally have confused and incorrect information regarding the relationship of food to body weight. The dietician's role is very important as she provides the anorectic with accurate nutritional information and works with the anorectic on issues related to her eating behavior. The anorectic learns from the dietician information about nutrition and about making appropriate food choices. The dietician will analyze the anorectic's current nutritional status and design an appropriate diet plan to increase her weight. The short term expected amount of weight gain will be continuously adjusted according to her caloric intake. The initial type of oral feeding depends on the severity of the anorectic's nutritional status. Her feedings may gradually progress from only liquids to soft foods, and eventually, regular food.

Food is given as if it were medicine with dosages prescribed on an individual basis. The process is initiated cautiously and caloric intake is progressively increased. Because the anorectic is extremely fearful of gaining weight, a gradual increase in caloric intake is better medically and psychologically. The dietician guides the anorectic toward gradual and controlled weight gain. She designs a diet which will consist of normal foods, some of which the anorectic would not eat prior to the onset of the disorder. Anorectics believe some foods, such as carbohydrates, sugar and meat, are intrinsically bad and unhealthy. The dietician suggests that the anorectic eat her "forbidden" foods in small quantities. During this process, the dietician tries to reduce the anorectic's anxiety associated with eating these foods.

If the anorectic fails to consume an adequate amount of the foods required and her weight drops, then she may be given an artificially prepared mixture, an oral supplement, which includes a concentrated source of nutrition in an easily digested and palatable form. In this supplement, her complete nutritional requirements can be supplied. If she is still resistant, she will be tube-fed until she reaches her previous weight.

Meals are served attractively and portions are gradually increased in size. By slowly increasing the size of the meals, time is provided for the anorectic to overcome the anxiety associated with eating. When she gains a certain amount of weight and her eating patterns are more normal, the dietician discusses with the anorectic the level of weight appropriate for her age, sex and height. The long term treatment goal is to reach the normal weight level specified in the behavioral contract. It has been found that anorectics improve if they also have knowledge about their progress during the behavior treatment program.[52] They are given information concerning the size of their meals, the number of calories they consume, the amount of their weight change, as well as their exact weight. Anorectics may monitor their own food intake, such as counting the number of mouthfuls they have eaten, or plotting graphs of their daily weight gain. These behaviors allow the anorectic to feel some control over her situation.

Nurse

The nurse's ability to establish rapport and a relationship of trust with the anorectic is an important variable to the success of treatment. Nurses usually monitor the anorectic's weight gain and her mealtime behavior. They are sensitive to the anorectic's terror of weight gain. Nurses supervise the anorectic as she eats her meals. The nurse observes the anorectic's eating behavior and makes helpful therapeutic interventions. Throughout the treatment processes, nurses continuously reassure the anorectic that she will not become too fat by following the hospital's diet plan.

ANORECTIC'S BEHAVIOR

The anorectic fights the hospital staff every inch of the way. She tries every possible maneuver to sabotage the staff's attempts to increase her weight. For example, large amounts of water may be consumed to increase weight immediately before weigh-ins. Others put heavy objects in their pockets. They may wear several pairs of socks, panties, and shoes in order to increase their weight. Many programs prevent the anorectics from preparing in advance for the weigh-ins by weighing at irregular times and without the anorectic having any prior notice of the exact time for the weigh-in.

If the anorectic is on forced tube feedings, she will pull out the intravenous tube and declare that it accidentally fell out. Oftentimes, as a result of these behaviors, the anorectic will be forceably restrained during the tube feeding procedure. Anorectics are extremely critical, and antagonize the entire staff. They constantly complain about the quality and type of foods which they are given. The food is either too hot or too cold. They criticize the nurses as being too strict. Anorectics try to manipulate one staff member against the other. They will try to vomit secretly, hide food, and then dispose of it. Yet, they will insist that they are not vomiting.

Anorectics frequently subject the hospital staff to angry outbursts and attacks. The anorectic views the staff's offer of help as hostile, intrusive, and coercive. When the anorectic fails to meet the criterion to receive her privilege, she may plead and beg that she still be given the reward whether she has gained the weight or not. If the rules of the treatment plan are changed, the anorectic becomes furious with the new conditions and threatens to run away from the hospital.

Hospital staff demonstrate considerable skill in tolerating the anorectic's manipulative, deceptive and negativistic behavior. Staff members understand that the anorectic is mentally ill and that she is being controlled by irrational fears. They realize that the anorectic must constantly manage tremendous levels of anxiety associated with her weight gain. Her disruptive behavior is motivated by the desperation of her situation. She may panic when her weight approaches the level for normal weight. At this weight, her body takes on the appearance of a sexually mature adult and the implications of this event are frightening to the anorectic.

CRITICISMS OF BEHAVIOR THERAPY

Several different types of behavior therapy programs have been effective in facilitating rapid weight gain with many anorectics. Behavior therapy programs are best used as a way to bring on rapid weight gain during the anorectic's nutritional crisis. Behavior therapy techniques have demonstrated good results in the short term but long range benefits of behavioral treatment are questionable. They are often inadequate for maintenance of the anorectic's normal eating behavior and weight over the long term.

Another source of criticism of behavior therapy is that the staff is able to reinforce the anorectic's behaviors in a hospital setting, but when she returns to the same disturbed family environment, therapeutic gains are quickly lost. Family and friends find it extremely difficult to apply or withdraw rewards contingent upon the anorectic's behavior. It is necessary, therefore, to work therapeutically with the family to insure that the gains made in the hospital are maintained at home.

Behavior therapy focuses upon the anorectic's eating behavior and weight gain and not on her underlying psychological problems. Behavior therapy programs do not help the anorectic's emotional problems, and, therefore, repeat the same mistakes that the anorectic's parents have made with her. They try to induce the anorectic to conform using a system of reward and punishment, and make her weight the most important factor. Consequently, the anorectic concludes that the clinicians, similar to her parents, are not interested in her or her inner values, but only in her weight.[53]

Behavioral therapy techniques have been criticized for causing further psychological damage to the anorectic. For example, the anorectic may experience increased emotional turmoil as a result of feeling bribed by the clinicians into relinquishing control of their bodies and their lives. Critics claim that many apparently successful behavior therapy programs actually have been followed by an increase in the anorectic's physical and emotional deterioration, even suicidal behavior.[54]

CRITICISMS OF HOSPITAL TREATMENTS

Hospital treatment approaches have been criticized as being too authoritarian and in direct opposition to what the anorectic is trying to achieve; autonomy and control over her own body. Treatment programs which include enforced bed rest, sedation, and tube feedings are humiliating experiences for the anorectic. She constantly tries to assert her independence even if this means that she must openly defy the staff's authority. Tube feedings or forceable administration of medication negatively affect the anorectic's attitude toward the hospital, and her willingness to return once she is discharged. There may be a relationship between the anorectic's resistance to return to the hospital for further treatment and the high mortality rate associated with this illness.

Chapter 6

PSYCHOTHERAPY

A HOSPITAL TREATMENT program includes psychiatrists and psychologists who immediately begin to treat the anorectic for her underlying psychological disturbances along with her medical treatment. Physicians work together with psychologists, each understanding their respective role in the treatment process while still maintaining continuous awareness of the anorectic's overall condition. Each persons' role, physician and psychologist, is clearly defined which gives the anorectic little opportunity to manipulate staff members. In particular, the team approach frees the psychologist to focus on the anorectic's psychological problem while the physician assumes primary care for her medical and nutritional needs.

After the anorectic's life is out of danger, psychological treatment is initiated. Weight gain not only reduces the threat to her life, it improves her mental functioning so that she may participate in meaningful psychotherapy. The therapist takes into consideration the type of medical treatment that was used to restore her weight to normal levels and assesses whether this has had any damaging effect on her long term psychological adjustment. There are a variety of psychological treatment approaches which are used to explore the anorectic's underlying psychological problems and to change her abnormal eating behavior. These approaches include individual therapy, family therapy, art therapy, and group therapy.

Once the anorectic is out of physical danger, it is necessary to establish appropriate treatment goals according to her psychopathology. The therapist's major concern is how effective the treatment will be in maintaining a safe weight while working toward her long term psychological adjustment. The first part of her treatment in the hospital was aimed at her physical symptoms. Forced feeding or behavior therapy techniques

57

were used to normalize her eating pattern and to restore her weight. The psychologist's task is directed toward resolving her underlying emotional problems and helping her to find healthier solutions for her internal conflict.

INDIVIDUAL PSYCHOTHERAPY

Individual therapy must be designed specifically for each anorectic. The effects of the starvation and the weight loss give anorectics a similar physical appearance; however, there is considerable difference between anorectics regarding the pattern of their underlying psychological problems. The therapist tailors the treatment to meet the different needs of each anorectic. There are some common psychological themes and core issues, however, which are relevant to anorectics in general and which often become the dynamic issues of the therapeutic process. These include autonomy and independence from the family, establishing a female sexual identity, and low self-esteem.

Anorectic's Resistance

The anorectic does not want to be cured nor can she see any reason for psychological treatment. It is not typical that psychologists treat patients against their will. Therefore, psychologists face a situation in which they must help an unwilling patient. The anorectic presents herself as someone who does not need any offer of help. The gesture of therapeutic assistance is considered by the anorectic to be dangerous. She has achieved security through her behavior although it has distorted her perception of reality. Since she feels emotionally safe and thinner, any interference with her eating pattern makes her defensive. Her eating behavior is designed to avoid intolerable levels of anxiety associated with her particular conflicts. Each time the therapist suggests the necessity for eating and gaining weight, her anxiety level rises and so does her resistance. The more intense these behaviors appear, the more desperate is the anorectic. Each of these behaviors reflect her despair and emotional fragility. These behaviors are motivated by a frightened individual who is desperately holding onto her "psychic" life, perhaps at the expense of her "physical" life.

Therapeutic Alliance

The therapist's attitude toward the anorectic is essential to the success of the therapy. The sight of an anorectic, emaciated and weak, causes considerable stress for the therapist. The anorectic's firm insistence that she is perfectly healthy creates additional frustration in the therapist. The anorectic, initially, is angry and defiant. Her interpersonal battle for independence and control becomes associated with the therapist. She resists any treatment regarding the subject of her weight gain as she fears losing control over her body and her life. The therapist recognizes the anorectic's need for control, and by so doing, reacts to her provocations with understanding.

Prior to the satisfactory resolution of the anorectic's emotional problems it is crucial that the therapist achieve a constructive therapeutic alliance. The anorectic needs to view the therapist as someone who understands her situation. Most importantly, she needs to accept the responsibility to work with the therapist in order to try to understand the reasons which precipitated her symptoms. At the same time, part of the reason for her behavior is a powerful inner drive toward independence. This independence is contrary to the need to participate in a relationship of mutual dependency with the therapist. These inner clashes vacillate in the anorectic throughout the therapeutic process.

The anorectic is an extremely difficult patient to treat. Therapy is a new experience for her. Perhaps, for the first time, she has someone who listens to her and who accepts her contributions as meaningful. The therapist accepts her as a worthwhile individual and does not value her on the basis of her weight. The therapeutic relationship of the therapist with the anorectic is the most powerful force in the healing process.

The therapeutic process attempts to discover the underlying causes of her illness and to help her find a solution to her problems. For the therapist, it is her emotions and not her appetite which are the major focus of attention. Through an examination of her past, the patient gains insight into the motives behind her past behavior. The therapist tries to assist the anorectic in understanding why she attempts to cope with life through the use of food and weight control. Many anorectics believe that their lives have been controlled and directed by their parents. The therapeutic task is to uncover their feelings of ineffectiveness, and to give them the confidence that they can do something about their problems other than through food or weight loss.

During the therapy sessions, the anorectic's vulnerable emotional areas of conflict are exposed. This process creates in her considerable fear and anxiety. Her self-esteem is extremely fragile and it is a difficult therapeutic task to approach these areas of vulnerability. The anorectic tries to defend herself from feeling anxious by limiting her discussion to topics of food. The therapist, however, tries to detour her attention away from issues of food, weight and eating toward the exploration of her emotional problems.

A significant turning point in the course of therapy is when the anorectic begins to focus on her real emotional difficulties; interpersonal, family, and internal conflicts. It was much easier for her to deal with her small world of food which she had created. Changing from physical problems to concentrating on underlying problems places her on the road to recovery. She relinquishes her anorectic posture and begins to face the emotional crisis she previously denied. Most importantly, she learns to see herself as abnormal and unattractive in her low body weight. She recognizes that her fear of weight gain is a symbolic expression of more serious psychological problems. Still, it may take months, even years, of determined therapeutic effort to progress toward recovery.

ART THERAPY

In addition to individual therapy, the anorectic may participate in art therapy sessions. Art therapy provides the anorectic with the opportunity to become more sensitive to her inner self. She creates art work which originates within herself and is not under the control of others. Art, poetry and drama are expressive therapies. The anorectic conveys her emotional conflict through the use of "body language" by starving herself. This is a non-verbal form of psychological defense and symbolic communication. Art and painting are similar forms of a non-verbal communication. Through art mediums she can express her unconscious emotional conflicts and enhance her inner self-awareness.

GROUP THERAPY

Group therapy has also been used to help anorectics. Through the process of group therapy, anorectics share common problems and can identify with each other. They express their thoughts and feelings in an atmosphere of acceptance by their peers. Group therapy also provides the anorectic with an opportunity to practice newly acquired skills with other patients in a supportive emotional environment. She receives validation from other group members, and other patients serve as models of coping behavior. There are problems, however, with group therapy. Some anorectics continue to identify themselves as anorectic and express envy and jealousy over another group member's low weight. They can also learn, and teach one another various anorectic behaviors, such as vomiting and laxative abuse.[55] The group therapist recognizes the therapeutic difficulties with group therapy, and will establish group rules of behavior to prevent the potential negative consequences of group therapy.

FAMILY THERAPY

Most anorectics, because of their youth, are living at home during the onset of their illness. They will continue to be influenced by their parents and the home environment. In these situations, family therapy is provided as part of the treatment plan in addition to the other therapies. Clinicians believe that caution is necessary when describing characteristics of a "typical" anorectic family. Each family is different and these differences are taken into consideration during treatment. Another caution is warranted because the family's current characteristics may not truly be representative of the family prior to the anorectic's illness. The family is observed only after the onset of the illness, and it is difficult to determine to what degree their current behavior is a result of, or a contributing cause to, their daughter's anorexia nervosa. It is clear, however, that the entire family is disturbed by, and involved in, this tragic situation.

The anorectic's family gives the appearance of being happy and healthy, however, there are often serious difficulties underneath this apparent picture of harmony. Family values contribute to the development of anorexia nervosa, such as the importance of physical appearance, physical fitness, and dieting. The personality characteristics of her parents as well as interfamilial relationships play an important role in the development of the disorder.

Parental Background

In many cases, both the mother and father of the anorectic demonstrate some form of psychological disturbance. In particular, depression or alcoholism are present in at least one parent. Frequently, depression is associated with the mothers of anorectics and alcoholism is associated with the fathers.[56] It is not possible to determine to what extent these conditions existed prior to the emergence of anorexia nervosa in their daughter. However, the presence of these psychological problems in some of the parents of anorectics could contribute to the emotional problems associated with the development of anorexia nervosa. The outward appearance of both parents, however, is the epitome of normality.

Mothers of anorectics are often described as controlling, overprotective, and the major family disciplinarian. She is described as emphasizing her own sense of what is appropriate rather than considering her daughter's needs. Prior to the illness, the mother occupied the central, dominant position in the family. After the illness, the anorectic occupies the central position in the family, and she is in constant conflict with her mother.

To outsiders, the anorectic's father appears to be a strong male who holds considerable authority within the family, however, within the family he is usually a weak figure. Fathers are most often advocates of the family values for outward appearance, achievement, and physical fitness. During family therapy sessions the father is pushed into the background and is regarded as emotionally absent, weak, and passive. Although he appears to be a minor figure in the family, he plays a major role in the illness. An area of particular difficulty for some fathers of anorectics is the emergence of their daughter's sexuality and their emotional reaction to this situation.[57]

Family systems theory describes certain general characteristics and patterns of family interactions which are relevant to the families of anorectics. Families of anorectics are reported to possess various combinations of four family characteristics: 1) enmeshment, 2) overprotectiveness, 3) rigidity, and 4) low tolerance for conflict.[17] All families share the same characteristics but these characteristics are particularly exaggerated in the anorectic's family. The anorectic's family may emphasize one of the characteristics patterns of interacting, such as enmeshment, or rely on a combination of patterns. Family systems theory supports the premise that family organizations and behaviors are related to the development and maintenance of anorexia nervosa.

Enmeshment

Some families of anorectics are characterized as highly enmeshed. Enmeshed families consist of family members who are too close and overly involved with one another. This is a considerable amount of intrusion in each other's life which may not be viewed as unpleasant by family members. There are negative aspects associated with enmeshment. In a highly enmeshed family, family members' lives overlap and there is not sufficient autonomy between each other. Under these conditions, parents often try to control the anorectic and she is not encouraged toward autonomy.

The enmeshed style of family relationships is frequently found between the anorectic and one of her parents. Consequently, one parent is highly involved with the anorectic while the other parent is detached or distant from that relationship. It is more common to find the relationship to be closer between the anorectic and her mother, unless the father assumed the nurturing responsibility. In these cases, the anorectic may have a closer relationship with her father.[58]

Often an enmeshed relationship exists between the anorectic and one parent when the parents' marital relationship is poor. The marital relationship may not be described as argumentative, but rather as an apathetic relationship. When the anorectic is enmeshed with one parent, she becomes caught in the marital conflict. In this situation, her illness minimizes the marital conflict between the parents and may even serve to cement the parental marriage. One result of an enmeshed family environment is that individual members do not have a sufficient amount of autonomy. When closeness within the family is excessive, the daughter is more likely to experience fear of leaving the protection of her parents and living on her own. Consequently, family overprotection and intrusive concern restrict the anorectic's development of autonomy.

Scapegoating

The marital relationship of the anorectic's parents may be poor for a variety of reasons; most commonly, the reasons are sexual in nature. Their unaddressed conflicts are hidden below the surface of what appears to be a harmonious marriage. When the parents lack fulfillment from each other, they seek satisfaction in other areas. The father may seek fulfillment through alcohol or work while a depressed mother may seek fulfillment through the anorectic child.[59]

Parents of the anorectics unconsciously deny their marital difficulties and declare the anorectic to be the problem. When the family focuses on the life-threatening situation of the anorectic, all other problems are buried. Her parents, therefore, do not experience stress associated with their marriage because their problems find an outlet in the illness of the

anorectic child. In a real sense, the child is involved in the parental conflict and actually keeps the family together. Thus, family relationships
and parental behavior may unknowingly actively maintain and reinforce the starvation eating pattern of their anorectic daughter. The
anorectic receives reinforcement by the attention her parents focus on
her dieting and unusual eating behavior.

Rigidity

Families of anorectics are rigid and resistant to change. Consequently,
during the anorectic's adolescence, a period when growth and change is
necessary, the family has considerable difficulty. As a result of the parents'
difficulties in making this adjustment to the maturing of the adolescent
anorectic, they continue to treat her like a little child. In addition to rigidity, families of anorectics are characterized as intellectual and objective,
without much demonstration of warmth and positive feelings between
family members. There seems to be a lack of sensitivity to the emotional
needs of one another as well as a reluctance to deal with important emotionally charged issues within the family. Therefore, the family avoids
conflicts through circumstantial and intellectual discussions. Since they
lack the ability to negotiate their conflicts, they ignore them. One way the
conflicts between parents and children can be avoided is by focusing upon
the eating problems of their anorectic daughter.

Family Therapy

Family therapists focus the family's attention on their real problems,
the family structure. Family therapists interpret the anorectic's weight loss
as a plea for help in a disturbed family. They do not consider the illness to
be a problem of the anorectic, but a family problem. The problem does
not belong solely to the child; the whole family is responsible for the abnormal eating patterns. The goal of the family therapist is to identify the
dysfunctional alliance and interactions in the family. Other family issues
which emerge during therapy are problems related to the anorectic's dependency and separation from the family. These psychological family
problems have been unconsciously denied by all family members; they
have viewed the problem to reside only in their anorectic daughter.

The purpose of family therapy is to eliminate the stress on the anorectic and to bring the other family conflicts into the open. The therapist attempts to change the pathological family alliances toward more

appropriate interpersonal alliances. Family therapists often initiate their treatment by meeting with the anorectic and her family at a family "lunch" session. This provides the opportunity for the therapist to observe the interactions of the family members during an eating situation. The therapist will intervene pointing out their family interactions and increase each member's awareness and understanding of their behavior. The family can then begin to change the pattern of these interactions.

The therapist tries to release the parents from using their daughter's eating behavior as a way to solve their own conflicts. During the therapy sessions the family tends to focus the entire conversation on the topic of food and the anorectic's abnormal eating behavior. Once the family can disengage itself from the topic of food and the anorectic's physical problems and begins to recognize how these issues are related to underlying family problems, the family is on the road to recovery. The psychological issues of separation, independence, and sexuality are addressed during the therapy sessions. Through the process of treatment, the anorectic and her family will work together toward encouraging and supporting her autonomy. As the family problems are corrected, neither the anorectic nor her family will need her symptoms any longer.

Outpatient Family Therapy

Family therapy is generally started when the anorectic is in the hospital and continues after her discharge. Most therapists agree that it is necessary to correct the dysfunctional family environment prior to the anorectic's discharge. If this is not achieved, the anorectic will return to the same pathological family environment and the gains made in the hospital would be lost when she returns to the same family pressures.

The therapist helps the anorectic's parents understand the causes and meanings of the anorectic's behavior, and to deal with the guilt which they experience during the treatment process. Parents need guidance and direction in understanding their daughter's manipulative and secretive behavior. The anorectic has experienced secondary gains associated with her illness; the power and control she has over the lives of her parents as a result of her abnormal eating behavior. The therapist helps the parents to set reasonable limits on the anorectic's behavior. This is extremely difficult for the parents to put into practice as they fear that anything they might do will make their daughter's condition worse. Parents are discouraged from resorting to any negative punitive behaviors, such as criticizing or ridiculing their daughter. Throughout the family therapy treatment, the therapist stresses that the anorectic's symptoms are a family problem and that her illness serves a protective function for the entire family.

Parental Reaction to Family Therapy

When the anorectic's illness serves the pathological needs of the parents and family, the anorectic's improvement causes the marital problem to resurface. Consequently, their stress can no longer be blamed on the child; they must manage it for themselves. In some cases, this is too difficult a task for the parents. There are reports of anorectic's mothers experiencing nervous breakdowns and fathers experiencing anxiety attacks after their daughter improves.[60] Other times, as the anorectic begins to mature and to grow as a result of treatment, her separation from the family seems inevitable. This relization is too painful to confront and, as a consequence, some parents leave treatment.[58] There are families, however, who do well in the treatment process and the parent's hope and cooperation is maintained throughout the therapy.

Critics of Family Therapy

In a study conducted among fifty families of anorectics, it was found that family therapy was successful with 43 out of 50 families of anorectics. This success record using family therapy is extremely impressive. The range of time for collecting the follow-up results was from three months to four years after the completion of treatment.[61] Critics, however, assert that the anorectics in the family treatment study had characteristics which would give them a better prognosis prior to treatment. Fifty percent of the anorectics in the sample entered treatment approximately six months from the onset of weight loss. Thus the anorectic was seen early in the illness. All of the anorectics in the sample were below the age of eighteen. In general, the characteristics of an early age of onset and a short duration of illness, have been associated with good prognosis.[62] It is unclear how much of the success of family therapy can be accounted for by these factors rather than the treatment itself. There is general agreement among clinicians that if the anorectic is going to return to her family, family therapy is a necessary part of the anorectic's total treatment plan.

What lies in the anorectic's future after her discharge?

Chapter 7

AFTER THE HOSPITAL

OUTPATIENT THERAPY

MOST ANORECTICS eventually manage to gain enough weight to warrant consideration for discharge from the hospital, however, their treatment is not finished at the time of discharge. They require outpatient support which is directed toward resolving their psychological conflicts and problems in family relationships. During the course of the illness, the anorectic experiences periods of remission and exacerbation which further indicate the necessity for continuous outpatient treatment.

Many anorectics, unfortunately, do not develop sufficient self-awareness concerning their psychological problems and, therefore, do not comply with outpatient therapy. These anorectics continue to minimize their symptoms and do not believe that they need any professional help. Another reason for poor compliance to outpatient therapy is that many anorectics remember their hospital experience as a place of torture and humiliation. In some instances, anorectics cooperated with the hospital weight gain program only to assure their discharge. After discharge, they resume their abnormal eating behaviors.

Some hospitals arrange the anorectic's discharge contingent upon her remaining in outpatient therapy. The hospital clinicians negotiate an outpatient treatment contract with the anorectic and her parents prior to her discharge. The contract generally specifies that should the anorectic's weight fall below a certain level, she would automatically be readmitted to the hospital. Other hospital programs include the possibility of legally committing the anorectic to outpatient treatment just as they would for inpatient treatment.[63]

Treatment outcomes vary considerably for the victims of anorexia nervosa. Some anorectics recover and attain a complete resolution of their psychological problems. Others enter into a chronic course of the illness and remain at borderline weight levels. Anorectics may also develop a different type of eating disorder, bulimia or obesity. For a few anorectics, the outcome may be death as a result of physical complications associated with starvation or as a result of suicide.

RECOVERY

A substantial number of pre-adolescent anorectics develop anorexia nervosa as a single episode and achieve full recovery with the aid of family and individual psychotherapy, or even without psychological help.[64] There are considerable differences reported in the literature regarding the criteria used as indicators of the anorectic's recovery from the illness. Most clinicians support the view that the anorectic's weight must be stable and close to the general population norms for her height and age. Also, the anorectic should be eating a reasonably balanced diet and she should no longer resort to her anorectic behaviors, such as vomiting and purging. There is general concensus among therapists that in addition to her improvement in weight and the elimination of her abnormal eating behaviors, other factors must be taken into consideration in order to determine the extent of the anorectic's recovery. These additional criteria include resumption of her menstruation, the quality of her sexual and social adjustment, and the acquisition of a realistic body image.

Resumption of her menstruation in a regular cyclical pattern is an important criteria for recovery. Even though the anorectic's weight is within normal limits, there is often a delay of several months before menstruation begins. Following the start of her menstruation, the anorectic confronts the painful issue associated with her emerging sexuality. Her ability to make more adult sexual relationships is an indication of recovery. Approximately 47% of anorectics maintain active heterosexual relationships or marry.[65]

Another sign of recovery is the anorectic's ability to acquire a realistic body image. The distortion of her body image as too fat is a key factor in the perpetuation of her dieting behavior. The corrective change in her body image along with her desire to look after her own body, health and safety, are indications of recovery. The anorectic needs to be accepting of her weight gain, and needs to develop a sense of self-worth which is not dependent upon how much she weighs. Treatment which is aimed at treating underlying psychological problems and the long term course of the illness is effective in the recovery of approximately 20% of anorectics, and in preventing some deaths.[66] Thus, in some cases, although the anorectic may reach a point of severe emaciation, she can still live to function as a relatively normal adult.

CHRONICITY

Figures report that only one-third or one-half of anorectics fully recover.[25] Many others, despite intensive treatment, remain chronically ill. Between 25% to 50% of the anorectics suffer a recurrence of their symptomatic behavior within two years of their discharge.[67] These anorectics continue to experience difficulties in several areas of functioning: menstruation, sexual and social adjustment, body image and weight.

Even though some anorectics achieve normal weight levels, they still experience amenorrhea. Twelve out of forty patients in one study continued to have amenorrhea although they achieved normal body weight which would be supported by the critical weight hypothesis for resumption of their menstruation. These twelve anorectics evidenced more anorectic behaviors than those patients who had resumed their menstruation.[68]

Chronic anorectics continue to have difficulty relating to others. They experience anxiety when eating in the presence of others, and prefer to eat alone. They become extremely anxious in the company of others and, therefore, tend to avoid social situations. These anorectics are withdrawn from others, and lead miserable and lonely lives. They feel overwhelmingly inadequate at their work and, in addition, have tremendous social and family problems.

The majority of anorectics do not achieve a satisfactory level of sexual adjustment. Many remain sexually inhibited and avoid sexual relationships. They continue to have fears associated with their own sexuality and heterosexual relationships. Those anorectics who do marry generally have unstable marriages and accommodating husbands.

Other anorectics are able to gain weight but are still unable to evalute their body image realistically. Therefore, once out of the hospital, their abnormal dieting behavior is resumed. These anorectics are unlikely to maintain a mature body weight as long as they continue to overestimate their body image. Due to their low weights, they often live out the rest of their lives on the brink of physical death. They wage an unending battle with their own bodies to sustain a weight just barely over the danger line.

They continue to be sensitive to issues of weight. These anorectics fear that they will lose control and overeat, and, therefore, become fat. Some still continue to think about food all of the time. One author reviewed the outcome data from twelve different studies. The results indicated that over half of the subjects continued to have eating problems.[25] Many anorectics remain severely undernourished for years following their discharge, even though they remain in psychotherapy.

Obesity and Bulimia

While many chronic anorectics remain severely underweight, others develop another form of eating disorder, obesity or bulimia. Between one-quarter and one-third of anorectics who achieve a normal level of body weight after their hospitalization begin to eat compulsively to a point of reaching obesity.[69] Other anorectics experience considerable fluctuation in their weight. They experience stable weight during calm periods but when under emotional stress, they develop bulimia. These anorectics fail to maintain their dieting behavior and binge on thousands of calories. There is some question whether obesity and bulimia are not a consequence of the reinforcement the anorectic receives for overeating when she is in the hospital. Many programs require that the anorectic gain weight rapidly. In some situations, the anorectic must consume an enormous amount of food to increase her weight significantly. Under these conditions, the anorectic's eating behavior, which resembles bulimic binging, appears to be reinforced by the hospital regime.[69]

MORTALITY

The mortality rate associated with anorexia nervosa is one of the highest of the mental illnesses. Approximately 15% of adolescents with anorexia nervosa are victims of premature death due to starvation and its implications.[70] Deaths due to renal failure and cardiac failure are associated with her malnutrition. The reported mortality rate for anorectics varies according to different reporting techniques. A review of twelve different studies of anorectics reported a mortality rate of six percent from self-starvation.[25] In general, this figure may be an underestimate. Many anorectics do not remain in treatment. Their deaths are often recorded as a result of a medical complication and not as a result of anorexia nervosa, a psychological condition.

A few anorectics die as a result of suicide. The likelihood of suicide is greater among bulimarexics who experience more impulsivity and depression, particularly associated with their binging, vomiting and purging behavior. In these cases, the combination of the anorectic's psychological problems and her nutritional imbalance take their toll and she contemplates suicide. The suicide rate among anorectics is approximately 1% and this is low relative to other mental illnesses such as schizophrenia which is estimated to have a 4% to 5% suicide rate.[25] The majority of anorectics do not commit suicide, nor do they believe that their starvation will lead to their death. Anorexia nervosa is a wasting disease, and death in a large proportion of cases is directly a result of malnutrition.

PREVENTION VS. TREATMENT

Many gains have been made in the community regarding anorexia nervosa. Just a few years ago, anorexia nervosa was a closely guarded secret and source of family embarrassment. Today, many more victims seek treatment as a result of increased social recognition and acceptance of the disorder as a mental illness. Professionals, physicians and mental health practitioners are able to recognize the symptoms during the early stages of the disorder and this leads to greater success in treatment.

While psychological treatment has been beneficial for many victims of anorexia nervosa, for a larger number of anorectics treatment has not been successful. There are many variables which work against the probability of success in treatment. The anorectic is a difficult patient to manage as she is unable to recognize her illness and, therefore, does not accept treatment. If she has been hospitalized for the condition, she is extremely resistant to re-admission. The aversive aspects of some treatments may actually decrease the probability of the anorectic voluntarily cooperating with treatment in the future.

Anorexia nervosa is an extremely difficult disorder to treat successfully. Nonetheless, individual psychotherapy offers at least some hope for recovery. There are far too many anorectics to treat on an individual basis. While treatment is necessary, it is not a sufficient solution to the problem of anorexia nervosa.

One factor which has been consistently associated with a more favorable prognosis is a short duration time between the onset of symptoms and the initiation of therapy.[71] It is imperative, therefore, that anorectics be identified at a young age and that they receive treatment in the early stages of the illness. This can be accomplished by the collective efforts of society. Individuals need to be informed concerning the symptoms of the illness and be alert in identifying potential anorectics, particularly in the high risk age range of adolescence.

SCHOOL SETTING

The incidence of anorexia nervosa among adolescents and young adult women indicates that the disorder can be found among the student population in schools and college campuses. There are recent reports of cases of anorexia nervosa as early as in elementary school.[72] Educators, counselors and school personnel can play a vital role in the possible prevention of anorexia nervosa by including the topic in the curriculum. Informed adolescents may exercise more caution about their personal dietary habits and they may be the first to recognize the signs of the disorder among their peers. Anorexia nervosa can be appropriately included in several subject areas: health, home economics and physical education.

Health

Since nearly every middle school student will take a course in health, information about anorexia nervosa could well be included in units on mental health, self-esteem, grooming, physical appearance, physiological growth and development, and issues related to sexuality. Youngsters need to be intellectually prepared for the rapid bodily changes which will occur during their adolescence. The teenage girl should look forward rather than fear these changes as she advances toward physical sexual maturity.

Home Economics

Social concern about the danger of obesity, the number one adolescent physical problem, has lead to an over-emphasis of weight control in the home economics curriculum. Emphasis should also be placed upon the nutritional hazards associated with excessive dieting. The student should become informed about the effects of malnutrition, and the irreversible medical problems which develop from severe weight loss. Crash dieting and engaging in food fads which are typical behaviors of the adolescent sub-culture, need to be distinguished from the obsessive dieting behavior of the girl with anorexia nervosa.[27]

Physical Education

Current physical education programs place considerable emphasis on physical fitness. There is a close relationship between the philosphical principles of physical education and the symptoms of anorexia nervosa. The physical educator encourages youngsters to participate in physical exercise programs and to maintain normal body weight for improved health. While physical educators have a social responsibility to promote physical exercise as a value among students, they also have a social responsibility to inform youngsters of the dangers of exercising and dieting when these behaviors are carried to an extreme degree.

The Coach and Anorexia Nervosa

Youngsters with anorexia nervosa are often found on athletic teams. They are extremely competitive and their parents generally encourage athletic participation. Coaches often encourage youngsters to diet and lose weight in order to improve their athletic performances. One girl with anorexia nervosa reported the onset of the disorder was associated with the coach's recommendation that she lose weight to make the gymnastics team. A coach's recommendation to lose weight is not sufficient to explain the development of the disorder. The youngster was most likely predisposed toward anorexia nervosa before any recommendation was made for her to lose weight. This occurrence does illustrate, however, the importance which a vulnerable youngster may attach to a coach's suggestion. The athletic coach must observe the dieting behavior of their athletes and be alert to any youngster who deviates from the normal expectation for dieting behavior.

Identification of the Anorectic in the Classroom

Generally, parents are responsible for identifying emotional illness in their children. With anorexia nervosa, however, her parents are unable to recognize that their youngster suffers from a serious mental disorder because the early symptoms of anorexia nervosa are similar to the values the parents place upon physical appearance, shape, weight, and achievement. The anorectic's parents also attribute other signs of the disorder, such as negativism and body image self-consciousness, to typical adolescent behavior. Consequently, neither the youngster nor her parents recognize the behavior as symptomatic of a psychological disorder. Since the parents are not aware that their youngster has a mental illness, psychological intervention is likely to be sought too late. Teachers and counselors can provide a vital service to the parents and the afflicted youngster by identifying the disorder in the early stages, thus psychological treatment can begin before the medical complications become irreversible.

Other school personnel can also help by identifying the early stages of the disorder. Some of the anorexics' symptoms represent an exaggeration of behaviors characteristic of all adolescents. Educators who are informed about the disorder are able to differentiate the adolescent who is an anorectic from the more typical adolescent. A team consisting of the classroom teacher, school nurse, physical education teacher, counselor, and administrator have the resources to systematically investigate the youngster's overall behavior.

Loss of Weight

The most prominent early sign for the classroom teacher to observe is the youngster's attitude toward her loss of weight. If the youngster is suffering from anorexia nervosa, the teacher will notice that the youngster is unusually eager to talk about her diet. The youngster will say that she was too fat and needed to start dieting. She will be absorbed with the ideas that center around food and will appear to enjoy participating in her diet. In contrast, the youngster without anorexia nervosa would complain about having to be on a diet. She would be unhappy about restricting her total food intake and about depriving herself of the food she enjoys. She would also have a variety of interests and conversation topics and would not appear to be absorbed with ideas centering around food.

The contrasting attitude toward the weight loss and dieting between the non-anorectic and the anorectic can serve as a clue to the classroom teacher for referral or consultation with other school personnel who are in the position to help. The physical education teacher is in an advantageous position to recognize any loss of weight in a student since during physical education class students wear fewer clothes. In the event of noticing any abnormality, the teacher should consult the school nurse who will compare the child's previous height and weight records with her current weight status. The nurse can accurately confirm the teacher's view that the youngster may be underweight.

Hyperactivity

If the youngster is an anorectic, the teachers will observe an increase in the student's energy level. This can be misinterpreted by uninformed teachers as indicating that the student has an increased realization of the importance of education and achievement.[73] The youngster's hyperactivity is closely associated with an increasee in her desire for physical activity. The anorectic will work and exercise for hours without experiencing any apparent fatigue. The non-anorectic youngster who is on a diet will be less hyperactive and will complain about doing the necessary painful exercises in order to lose weight. She will feel fatigue and cease her physical activity.

The non-anorectic youngster will express concern and realize that she has lost too much weight. Her perceptions of her thin appearance will be consistent with the teacher's perceptions. This student will eliminate exercising and she will eat foods that will help her to gain some of her lost weight. If she continues to lose weight, the youngster recognizes that she has a medical problem and seeks medical advice.

Amenorrhea

Amenorrhea is also considered as early indicator of the disorder. The physical educator may have sufficient rapport with the youngster to discuss any menstrual irregularity. Girls often ask to be excused from physical education class as a result of menstrual problems. When the youngster without anorexia nervosa experiences the cessation of her menstruation, she typically talks about it and expresses her fears. She would realize that she has a physical problem and would seek medical advice. The school nurse also would be an appropriate person to gently inquire about the youngster's menstruation regularity and irregularity. The youngster with anorexia nervosa will not communicate any concern about her amenorrhea.

The Shift From Compliance to Negativism

The youngster with anorexia nervosa shifts from being a compliant student to a negativistic student. She is unable to maintain the quality of her school work. She argues with the teacher over a one point difference in her grade, and is highly sensitive to the teacher's criticism. The youngster with anorexia nervosa is particularly argumentative and stubborn concerning her dieting behavior. Adolescents in general rebel against authority in an effort to assert their independence. The adolescent without anorexia nervosa, however, would recognize the danger associated to her health by continuing to refuse to eat as being more important than her need to assert her independence. The healthy adolescent's judgement and concern about the amount of weight loss would override her concern for autonomy. At this time the typical adolescent would be receptive to parental, medical and teacher advice.

The Anorectic's Peers

The teacher or school counselor could have informal discussions with the classmates of the youngster suspected of having anorexia nervosa. Her peers may be the first to notice the anorectic's weight loss. They might notice her during their physical education class and observe how skinny she has become. Her peers would also observe the anorectic's bizarre eating habits at the lunch table and her incessant preoccupation with dieting and food. As the disorder progresses, the anorectic will have difficulty relating to others and will eventually withdraw from her peers.

Referral

When the classroom teacher, nurse, physical education teacher, and counselor suspect that the youngster's behavior is consistent with the signs of anorexia nervosa, they should present their findings to the school administrator. The administrator should invite her parents to attend a school conference. The administrator should be empathetic and understanding with the parents and should expect them to be resistant to any suggestion that their youngster may have psychological problems. The administrator should stress the importance of an examiniation of the youngster by a physician and a clinical psychologist or a psychiatrist. If necessary, the administrator should insist that a psychological evaluation be completed in order for the child to remain in school. The administrator may request some notification from the physician assuring the school that there will be no danger to her health if she remains in school. The administrative pressure could be the first step toward reversing the progress of this serious mental illness. Early identification of youngsters with anorexia nervosa increases the likelihood of a more favorable prognosis. Early psychological treatment may spare the parents and the affected youngster the agony and suffering associated with the final stages of this devasting disorder.

SOCIAL FORCES

It is not enough to include the topic of anorexia nervosa in the educational curriculum nor to train teachers in the early identification of potential victims. Women in society need to examine the relationship between society's current values of dieting and exercising and the high incidence of the disorder among women. The symptoms of anorexia nervosa are clear examples of the relationship between social values and mental illness. Another mental illness, hysteria, predominantly affected women during the Victorian period, and was also influenced by social conditions.

Hysteria

Freud's early patients were vitims of hysteria. These women displayed behaviors, such as dependence and helplessness, which were stereotypical behaviors of women during the nineteenth century. Similarly, the anorectic's symptoms of dieting and weight consciousness, reflect characteristics typical of women in contemporary society. The symptoms of both disorders reflect socially approved female behaviors.

Freud demonstrated a relationship between the incidence of hysteria and the punitive aspects of the sexually repressive Victorian society. Over a period of time, social values have changed toward a freer expression of sexuality and the incidence of hysteria decreased. Freud directed his treatment not only to the afflicted individual but to society at large. The incidence of anorexia nervosa, similarly, may decrease by changing social values which are specifically relevant to women in today's society. The prevention of anorexia nervosa is the collective responsibility of everyone in society.

A Thin Body Ideal

A rise in the incidence of anorexia nervosa is related to unrealistic social pressure for women to alter their different bodies into one shape, a thin body ideal. Women are extremely self-conscious about their physi-

cal appearance. They can feel devastated by the addition of a few un-
noticeable pounds. Women constantly view themselves as overweight
and inferior when comparing themselves to a thin body standard of
beauty. Women do not determine their own definition of beauty.
Fashion, dieting, and physical fitness industries package beauty in products and then sell these products to women. Women purchase
sportswear, sneakers, and aerobic video tapes to exercise away extra
pounds. Millions of women purchase diet aids, diet foods, and diet cookbooks. The major consumers of fitness and dieting products are women.
The health industry also prescribes dieting and exercising as essential to
maintain or improve a woman's health. Women need to challenge these
diet and fitness prescriptions. Current evidence suggests that the recommendation to decrease saturated fats and increase physical activity is
controversial.[74] Many medical authorities agree that it is healthier to be
a little overweight then underweight, unless the individual has diabetes,
high serum lipid cholesterol, or high blood pressure.[75]

Social pressures to be physically fit and to achieve a thin figure lead
women to an obsession with dieting. Dieting is so commonplace that it is
difficult to differentiate potential anorectics from healthier women. Eating disorders may be on a continuum from problem-free to anorectic-like
behavior and then to anorexia nervosa.[25] Anorectic-like behaviors which
are reported by women include binging and vomiting. So many women
indulge in vomiting that it is difficult to persuade them that it is not just
another weight control method. Binge eating behavior is a problem which
may be reaching epidemic proportions. Individuals of normal and obese
weight levels report a pattern of weight control which includes binging,
dieting and purging behavior. There are estimates that as many as 35%
to 60% of college women are considered to be binge eaters.[76]

Dieting is a constant topic of conversation among women. Women
receive social acceptance and approval for their dieting behavior. Not
only do they share appropriate nutritional ideas and information on
dieting, they teach each other self-induced vomiting techniques. Many
women who do resort to vomiting for weight control report that they
were taught how to vomit deliberately by another woman.[77]

All women must come to realize that vomiting and laxative abuse are
not regarded as "tools" of successful dieters; they are dangerous pathological behaviors. Women resort to these behaviors because they fear that
they are fat when they are not overweight. The prevalence of fasting,
vomiting and binging behavior among women suggests a high percentage of the population engage in anorectic-like dieting behaviors. These

women, however, do differ from anorectics. Women with anorectic-like behavior were better adjusted academically, sexually and socially, while the anorectic is severely impaired in all areas of functioning.[77] While there are many examples of women who report anorectic-like behaviors, a causal relationship between their behavior and the development of anorexia nervosa has not been clinically established. Some may fall victim to anorexia nervosa while others may not.

Social pressures for women to be thin and physically fit contribute to the expression of the disorder in vulnerable young girls and women. Socio-cultural factors alone would not sufficiently explain the development of the disorder, however, the symptoms can be understood when viewed in the context of current social values and attitudes. Social values for women need to be kept in proper perspective. Dieting and physical fitness have a place within the health system of our society, however, they have achieved too much social importance and endorsement. Women are extremely self-conscious about their body shape. Women must challenge any definition of beauty which is tied to their physical shape. A woman must not yield to social pressures which objectify her value as a "body." Instead women need to create their own definition of womanhood based on an internal value system.

EARLY INTERVENTION

Another important social responsibility is the identification of potential anorectics in the population. The earlier the anorectic can be identified in the course of the illness and brought to treatment, the more favorable is her prognosis as the medical complications are still reversible. The disorder must be recognized early and she must be treated early in the illness. As the disorder advances, the anorectic is likely to reach a stage of nutritional crisis and she would be subjected to aversive forced feeding techniques.

Educators, parents, friends and relatives must act immediately if they suspect that the young girl is anorectic. When this occurs, parents must immediately take their child to a physician and a psychologist. The most dangerous position to take is to assume that she has only a simple eating problem, and that in a short time it will go away. Any lapse of time will help the symptoms of anorexia nervosa to become firmly rooted and lessen the young girl's chances for recovery, and could become fatal.

SOURCES OF INFORMATION IN THE COMMUNITY

There are community organizations which offer considerable support and information to anorectics and their family. Many of these organizations publish newsletters concerning anorexia nervosa as well as bulimia. These agencies are a valuable resource not only to the afflicted individual, but to professionals as well. The following list includes the names and addresses of some of these helpful organizations:

AMERICAN ANOREXIA/BULIMIA ASSOCIATION, INC.

133 Cedar Lane
Teaneck, New Jersey 07666

ANOREXIA NERVOSA AND RELATED EATING DISORDERS, INC.

P.O. Box 5102
Eugene, Oregon 97405

NATIONAL ASSOCIATION OF ANOREXIA NERVOSA AND ASSOCIATED DISORDERS, INC.

Box 271
Highland Park, Illinois 60035

THE CENTER FOR THE STUDY OF ANOREXIA AND BULIMIA

Institute for Contemporary Psychotherapy
1 West 91st Street
New York, New York 10024

ANOREXIC AID

The Priory Centre
11 Priory Road
High Wycombe, Bucks

FOOTNOTES

1. Jones, Dolores, J., Fox, Mary M., Babigian, Harovtun, M., and Hutton, Heide E.: Epidemiology of anorexia nervosa in Monroe County, New York: 1960-1976, *Psychosomatic Medicine*, *42*(6):551, November 1980.
2. Swift, William, Jr.: The long-term outcome of early onset anorexia nervosa: a critical review. *Journal of the American Academy of Child Psychiatry*, *21*(1):45, January 1985. From Greenfield, N.: *Personal Communication*, 1980.
3. *Diagnostic and Statistical Manual of Mental Disorders* (Third Edition), The American Psychiatric Association, 68, 1980.
4. Irwin, Martin: Diagnosis of anorexia nervosa in children and the validity DSM III. *American Journal of Psychiatry*, *138*(10):1382, October 1981.
5. Launer, M. A.: Anorexia nervosa in late life. *British Journal of Medical Psychology*, *5*(4):375, December 1978.
6. Piazza, E., Piazza, N., and Rollins, N.: Anorexia nervosa: controversial aspects of therapy. *Comprehensive Psychiatry*, *21*(3):178, May/June 1980.
7. Lewis, Carol R.: Elizabeth Barrett Browning's family disease, anorexia nervosa. *Journal of Marital and Family Therapy*, *8*(1):129, January 1982.
8. Ross, Jack L.: Anorexia nervosa: an oveview. *Bulletin of the Menninger Clinic*, *41*(5):419, September 1977.
9. Anorexia, the "starving disease" epidemic, *U. S. News and World Report*, *47*, August 30, 1982.
10. Crisp, A. H., Hsiu, L. K., Chen, C.N., Wheeler, M.: Reproductive hormone profiles in male anorexia nervosa before, during and after restoration of body weight to normal. *International Journal of Eating Disorders*, *1*(3):9, Spring 1982.
11. McDermott, Barry: The glitter has gone. *Sports Illustrated*, 57(2):94, November 8, 1982.
12. Crisp, A. H., Hsu, L. K. G., Harding, Britta, and Hartshorn, J.: Clinical features of anorexia nervosa. *Journal of Psychosomatic Research*, *24*:182, 1980.
13. Papalla, Anthony and Bode, Jacqueline: Perspectives on the anorectic student. *Journal of College Student Personnel*, pp. 224-228, May 1981.
14. Halmi, Katherine A.: Anorexia nervosa: Demographic and clinical features in 94 cases. *Psychosomatic Medicine*, *36*(1):23, January-February, 1974-75.
15. Casper, Regina C., and Davis, John M.: On the course of anorexia nervosa. *American Journal of Psychiatry*, 134(9):975, September 1977.

16. Russell, Gerald: Bulimia nervosa: an ominous variant of anorexia nervosa. *Psychological Medicine*, 9:437, 447, 1979.
17. Shiner, Gail: Anorexia nervosa studied at several centers. *Research Resources Reporter*, 5:6, May 1980.
18. Seligmann, J., Zabarsky, M., Witherspoon, D., Rotenbeck, L., and Schmidt, Mireya: A deadly feast and famine. *Newsweek*: 60, March 7, 1983.
19. Corliss, Richard: The new ideal of beauty. *Time*, 77: August 30, 1982.
20. Goldblatt, P. B., Moore, M.E., and Slunkard, A. L.: Social factors and obesity, *Journal of American Medical Associations*, 192:1039, 1965.
21. Garner, David M., Garfinkel, Paul E., Schwartz, Donald, and Thompson, Michael: Cultural expectations of thinness in women. *Psychological Reports*, 47:483, 484, 489, 1980.
22. Wooley, O. Wayne and Wooley, Susan: The Beverly Hills eating disorder: the mass marketing of anorexia nervosa. *International Journal of Eating Disorders*, 11(3):67, Spring 1982.
23. Stern, Judith, S.: Weight control programs. Winick, Myron: *Nutritional Disorders of Women*, New York, Wiley & Sons, 1977, pp. 137.
24. Alford, Betty H., and Bogle, Margaret L.: *Nutrition During the Life Cycle*, Englewood Cliffs, Prentice-Hall, 1982, pp.218.
25. Schwarz, Donald M., Thompson, Michael G., and Johnson, Craig L.: Anorexia nervosa and bulimia: the social-cultural context. *International Journal of Eating Disorders*, 1(3):22, 29, Spring 1982.
26. Kay, Elizabeth: On starving oneself to death. *Family Health*, 40, pp. 28, September 1979.
27. Wesley, Myrna M., Ruddy, R. D., and Susan Gibson Ruddy: Anorexia nervosa: an obsession with thinness. *Forecast for Home Economics*, 119, September 1981.
28. Bromberg, D., Commins, S., and Friedman, S. B.: Protecting physical and mental health. In Rehage, Kenneth J., *Toward Adolescence: the Middle School Years, Seventy-Ninth Yearbook of the National Society for the Study of Education*. Chicago, NSSE, 1980, Chapter VIII, pp. 137.
29. Winick, Myron, M. D., *Nutrition in Health and Disease*, New York, Wiley & Sons, 1980, pp. 21.
30. Dwyer, Johanna T., Feldman, Jacob J., and Mayer, Jean: The social psychology of dieting. Harvard School of Public Health, 269:271.
31. Douvan, Elizabeth: Sex differences in the opportunitites, demands, and developments of youth. In Rehage, Kenneth J.: *The Seventy-Fourth Yearbook of the National Society for the Study of Education*. Chicago, NSSE, 1975, Chapter II, pp. 28.
32. Mitchell, Diane: Anorexia nervosa. *Arts in Psychotherapy*, 7(1):57, 1980.
33. Blos, Peter: The second individuation process of adolescence. *Psychoanalytic Study of the Child*, 22:174, 1967.
34. Freud, Anna: Adolescence. *Psychoanalytic Study of the Child*, 13:258, 1958.
35. Casper, Regina C., Halmi, Katherine A., Goldberg, Solomon C., Eckert, Elke D., and Davis, John M.: Disturbances in body image estimation as related to other characteristics and outcome in anorexia nervosa. *British Journal of Psychiatry*, 134:60, 1979.

36. Holt, S., Ford, M. J., Grant, S., and Heading, R. C.: Abnormal gastric empty-ing in primary anorexia nervosa. *British Journal of Psychiatry, 139*:550, 1980.

37. Brambilla, F., Cocchi, D., Nobile, P., and Miller, Eugenio E.: Anterior pi-tuitary responsiveness to hypothalamic hormones in anorexia nervosa. *Neuropsy-chobiology, 7*:234, 1981.

38. Leon, Gloria R.: Anorexia nervosa: the question of treatment emphasis in Ro-senbaum, M., Franks, C. M., and Yaffe, Y.: *Perspectives in Behavior Therapy,* New York, Springer Publishing Co., 1983, pp. 364.

39. Crisp, A. H.: Some psychobiological aspects of adolescent growth and their rele-vance for the fat/thin syndrome (anorexia nervosa). *International Journal of Obesity, 1*:232, 1977.

40. Katz, J. L., Weiner, H.: The aberrant reproductive endocrinology of anorexia nervosa in Weiner, H., Hofer, M. A., Stunkard, A. J., Eds.: New York, Raven Press, 1980, pp. 165.

41. Keys, A., Brozek, J., Henschel, A., Mickelsen, O., and Taylor, H. L.: *The Biology of Human Starvation,* Minneapolis, University of Minnesota, 1950, vol 1, pp. 900-918.

42. Green, R. S., and Rau, J. H.: Treatment of compulsive eating disturbances with anticonvulsant medication. *American Journal of Psychiatry, 131*(4):428, April 1974.

43. Lupton, M., Simon, L., Barry, V., and Klawans, H. L.: Biological aspects of anorexia nervosa. *Life Sciences, 18*:1342, 1976.

44. Climo, L. H.: Anorexia nervosa associated with hypothalamic tumor: the search for clinical-pathological correlations. *de psychiatrie de l'Univ. d'Ottawa, 7*(11):20, March 1982.

45. Sours, J. A.: The anorexia nervosa syndrome: phenomenologic and psycho-dynamic components. *Psychiatric Quarterly, 43*:240, 1969.

46. Russell, Gerald: The current treatment of anorexia nervosa. *British Journal of Psy-chiatry, 138*:165, 1981.

47. Browning, Charles H.: Anorexia nervosa: complications of somatic therapy. *Comprehensive Psychiatry, 18*(4):402, July/August 1977.

48. Pertschuk, M. J., Forster, J., Buzby, G., and Mullen, J. L.: The treatment of anorexia nervosa with total parenteral nutrition. *Biological Psychiatry, 167*(6):540, June 1981.

49. Werry, J. S., and Bull, D.: Anorexia nervosa: a case study using behavior therapy. *Journal of American Academy of Child Psychiatry, 14*(4):648, Autumn 1975.

50. Agras, S., Barlow, D. H., Chapin, H. N., Abel, G., and Leitenberg, H.: Be-havior modification of anorexia nervosa. *Arch Gen Psychiatry, 30*:279, March 1974.

51. Blinder, B. J., Freeman, D. M. A., and Stunkard, A. J.: Behavior therapy of anorexia nervosa: effectiveness of activity as a reinforce of weight gain. *American Journal of Psychiatry, 126*:1093, 1970.

52. Monte, P. M., McCrady, B. S., Barlow, D. H.: Effect of positive re-inforcement: informational feedback and contingency contracting on bulimic anorexic female. *Behavior Therapy, 8*(2):258, March 1977.

53. Lawrence, Marilyn: Anorexia nervosa: the counsellor's role. *British Journal of Guidance,* 9(1):78, January 1981.
54. Bruch, Hilde: Perils of behavior modification in treatment of anorexia nevosa. *Journal of the American Medical Association,* 230(10):1422, 1974.
55. Polivy, Janet: *Group Therapy for Anorexia Nervosa.* Toronto, University of Toronto and Clarke Institute of Psychiatry, 1979, pp. 1.
56. Strober, Michael: The significance of bulimia in juvenile anorexia nervosa: an exploration of possible etiologic factors. *International Journal of Eating Disorders,* 1(1):41, Fall 1981.
57. Anrewartha, Graham: Anorexia nervosa: three case studies of TA treatment. *Transactional Analysis Journal,* 12(2):110, April 1982.
58. Kalucy, R. S., Crisp, A. H., and Harding, Britta: A study of 56 families with anorexia nervosa. *British Journal of Medical Psychology,* 50(4):394, December 1977.
59. Yager, Joel: Family issues in the pathogenesis of anorexia nervosa. Psychosomatic Medicine, 44(1):44, March 1982.
60. See, Carolyn: Anorexia nervosa is starvation by choice. *Today's Health*:50, May 1975.
61. Minuchin, Salvador, Rosman, B. L., Baker, L.: *Psychosomatic Families: Anorexia Nervosa in Context,* 6th ed., Cambridge, Harvard University Press, 1982.
62. Garfinkel, Paul E., Garner, David M., and Moldofsky, Harvey: The role of behavior modification in the treatment of anorexia nervosa. *Journal of Pediatric Psychology,* 2(3):118, 1977.
63. Whipple, Stephan B., and Manning, Donald E.: Anorexia nervosa: commitment to a multifaceted treatment program. *Psychotherapy and Psychosomatics,* 30(3-4):167, 1978.
64. Pierloot, R., Vandereycken, W., Verhaest, S.: An inpatient treatment program for anorexia nervosa patients. *Acta Psychiatrica Scandinavica,* 66(1):7, July 1982.
65. Larson, R., and Johnson C.: Anorexia nervosa in the context of daily experience. *Journal of Youth and Adolescence,* 10(6):456, December 1981.
66. Crisp, A. H.: Therapeutic outcome in anorexia nervosa: *Canadian Journal of Psychiatry,* 26(4):232, June 1981.
67. Moldofsky, H., and Garfinkel, P. E.: Problems of treatment of anorexia nervosa. *Canandian Psychiatric Association Journal,* 19:169, 1974.
68. Falk, James R., and Halmi, Katherine A.: Amenorrhea in anorexia nervosa; examination of the critical body weight hypothesis. *Biological Psychiatry,* 17(7):799, 1982.
69. Bemis, Kelly M.: Current approaches to the eliology and treatment of anorexia nervosa. *Psychological Bulletin,* 85(3):604, 1978.
70. Clark, Duncan B., Mumford, Paul R.: Behavioral consultation to pediatrics. *Child Behavior Therapy,* 2(3):26, Fall 1980.
71. Becker, H., Korner, P., and Staffer, A.: A study of family dynamics and prognosis. *Psychotherapy and Psychosomatics,* 36(1):15, 1981.
72. Ceaser, Martin: Hunger in primary anorexia nervosa. *American Journal of Psychiatry,* 136(7):979-980, July 1979.
73. Sours, John A., M.D., *Starving to Death in a Sea of Objects.* New York, Jason Arson, 1980, pp. 187.

74. Singer, Jerome E., and Krantz, David S.: Perspectives on the interface between psychology and public health. *American Psychologist, 37*(8):959, August 1982.

75. McNurlen, Carolyn A., Anorexia nervosa: is the family to blame? Can the family help? *Better Homes and Gardens*:68, May 1985.

76. Rodin, Judith: A sense of control. *Psychology Today,* December 1984, pp. 43.

77. Thompson, Michael G., and Schwartz, Donald M.: Life adjustment of women with anorexia nervosa and anorexic-like behavior. *International Journal of Eating Disorders, 1*(2):58, Winter 1982.

BIBLIOGRAPHY

1. Adrewartha, Graham: Anorexia nervosa: three case studies of TA treatment. *Transactional Analysis Journal, 12*(2):110, April 1982.
2. Agras, S., Barlow, D. H., Chapin, H. N., Abel, G. and Leitenberg, H.: Behavior modification of anorexic nervosa. *Arch Gen Psychiatry, 30*:279, March 1974.
3. Alford, Betty H., and Bogle, Margaret L.: *Nutrition During the Life Cycle*, Englewood Cliffs, Prentice-Hall, 1982, pp. 218.
4. Anorexia, the "starving disease" epidemic, *U. S. News and World Report, 47*, August 30, 1982.
5. Becker, H., Korner, P., and Staffer, A.: A study of family dynamics and prognosis. *Psychotherapy and Psychosomatics, 36*(1):15, 1981.
6. Bemis, Kelly M.: Current approaches to the eliology and treatment of anorexia nervosa. *Psychological Bulletin, 85*(3):604, 1978.
7. Blinder, B. J., Freeman, D. M. A., and Stunkard, A. J.: Behavior therapy of anorexia nervosa: effectiveness of activity as a reinforcement of weight gain. *American Journal of Psychiatry, 126*:1093, 1096, 1970.
8. Blos, Peter: The second individuation process of adolescence. *Psychoanalytic Study of the Child, 22*:174, 1967.
9. Brambilla, F., Cocchi, D., Nobile, P., and Miller, E.: Anterior pituitary responsiveness to hypothalamic hormones in anorexia nervosa. *Neuropsychobiology, 7*:234, 1981.
10. Bromberg, D., Commins, C., and Friedman, S. B.: Protecting physical and mental health. In Rehage, Kenneth J., *Toward Adolescence: The Middle School Years, Seventy-Ninth Yearbook of the National Society for the Study of Education*. Chicago, NSSE, 1980, Ch. VIII, pp. 137.
11. Browning, Charles H.: Anorexia nervosa: complications of somatic therapy. *Comprehensive Psychiatry, 18*(4):402, July/August 1977.
12. Bruch, Hilde: Perils of behavior modification in treatment of anorexia nervosa. *Journal of the American Medical Association, 230*(10):1422, 1974.
13. Casper, Regina C., and Davis, John M.: On the course of anorexia nervosa. *American Journal of Psychiatry, 134*(9):975, September 1977.
14. Casper, R., Halmi, K., Goldberg, S. C., Eckert, E. D., and Davis, J. M.: Disturbances in body image estimation as related to other characteristics and outcome in anorexia nervosa. *British Journal of Psychiatry, 134*:60, 1979.

15. Ceaser, Martin: Hunger in primary anorexia nervosa. *American Journal of Psychiatry, 136*(7):979-980, July 1979.
16. Clark, Duncan B., Mumford, Paul R.: Behavioral consultation to pediatrics. *Child Behavior Therapy, 2*(3):26, Fall 1980.
17. Climo, L. H.: Anorexia nervosa associated with hypothalmic tumor: the search for clinical-pathological correlations. *de psychiatrie de l'Univ. d'Ottawa, 7*(11):20, March 1982.
18. Corliss, Richard: The new ideal of beauty. *Time,* 76, 77, August 30, 1982.
19. Crisp, A. H.: Some psychobiological aspects of adolescent growth and their relevance for the fat/thin syndrome (anorexia nervosa). *International Journal of Obesity, 1*:232, 1977.
20. Crisp, A. H.: Therapeutic outcome in anorexia nervosa: *Canadian Journal of Psychiatry, 26*(4):232, June 1981.
21. Crisp, A. H., Hsiu, L. K., Chen, C. N., Wheeler, M.: Reproductive hormone profiles in male anorexia nervosa before, during and after restoration of body weight to normal. *International Journal of Eating Disorders, 1*(3):9, Spring 1982.
22. Crisp, A. H., Hsiu, L. K., Harding, B., and Hartshorn, J.: Clinical features of anorexia nervosa. *Journal of Psychosomatic Research, 24*:182, 1980.
23. *Diagnostic and Statistical Manual of Mental Disorders* (Third Edition), The American Psychiatric Association, 1980, pp. 68.
24. Douvan, Elizabeth: Sex differences in the opportunities, demands, and development of youth. In Rehage, Kenneth J.: *The Seventy-Fourth Yearbook of the National Society for the Study of Education.* Chicago, NSSE, 1975, Ch. II, pp. 28.
25. Dwyer, J. T., Feldman, J. J., and Mayer, J.: The social psychology of dieting. *Harvard School of Public Health, 269*:271.
26. Falk, J. R., and Halmi, K. A.: Amenorrhea in anorexia nervosa; examination of the critical body weight hypothesis. *Biological Psychiatry, 17*(7):799, 1982.
27. Freud, Anna: Adolescence. *Psychoanalytic Study of the Child,* 1958, vol. 13, pp. 258.
28. Garfinkel, P. E., Garner, D. M., and Moldofsky, H.: The role of behavior modification in the treatment of anorexia nervosa. *Journal of Pediatric Psychology, 2*(3):118, 1977.
29. Garner, D. M., Garfinkel, P. E., Schwartz, D. and Thompson, M.: Cultural expectations of thinness in women. *Psychological Reports, 47*:483, 484, 489, 1980.
30. Goldblatt, P. B., Moore, M. E., and Slunkard, A. L.: Social factors and obesity, *Journal of American Medical Association, 192*:1039, 1965.
31. Green, R. S., and Rau, J. H.: Treatment of compulsive eating disturbances with anticonvulsant medication. *American Journal of Psychiatry, 131*(4):428, April 1974.
32. Halmi, Kathreine A.: Anorexia nervosa: demographic and clinical features in 94 cases. *Psychosomatic Medicine,* vol. XXXVI, no. 1, January/February 1974-75, pp. 23.
33. Holt, S. Ford, M. J., Grant, S., and Heading, R. C.: Abnormal gastric emptying in primary anorexia nervosa. *British Journal of Psychiatry, 139*:550, 1980.
34. Irwin, Martin: Diagnosis of anorexia nervosa in children and the validity DSM III. *American Journal of Psychiatry, 138*(10):1382, October 1981.

35. Jones, Dolores J., and Fos, Mary M.: Epidemiology of anorexia nervosa in Monroe County, New York, 1960-1976. *Psychosomatic Medicine*:551, November 1980.
36. Kalucy, R. S., Crisp, A. H., and Harding, B.: A study of 56 families with anorexia nervosa. *British Journal of Medical Psychology, 50*(4):394, December 1977.
37. Katz, J. L., Weiner, H.: The aberrant reproductive endocrinology of anorexia nervosa in Weiner, H., Hofer, M., Stunkard, A., (Eds.): New York, Raven Press, 1980, pp. 165.
38. Kay, Elizabeth: On starving oneself to death. *Family Health, 40*:28, September 1979.
39. Keys, A., Brozek, J., Henschel, A., Mickelsen, O., and Taylor, H. L.: *The Biology of Human Starvation*, Minneapolis, University of Minnesota, 1950, vol. 1, pp. 900-918.
40. Larson, R., and Johnson, C.: Anorexia nervosa in the context of daily experience. *Journal of Youth and Adolescence, 10*(6)456: December 1981.
41. Launer, M. A.: Anorexia nervosa in late life. *British Journal of Medical Psychology, 5*(4):375, December 1978.
42. Lawrence, Marilyn: Anorexia nervosa: the counsellor's role. *British Journal of Guidance, 9*(1):78, January 1981.
43. Leon, Gloria R., Anorexia nervosa: the question of treatment emphasis. Um, M., Franks, C. M., and Yaffe, Y.: *Perspectives in Behavior Therapy*, New York, Springer Publishing Co. 1983, pp. 364.
44. Lewis, Carol R.: Elizabeth Barrett Browning's family disease, anorexia nervosa. *Journal of Marital and Family Therapy, 8*(1):129, January 1982.
45. Lupton M., Siomon, L., Barry, V., and Klawans, H. L.: Biological aspects of anorexia nervosa. *Life Sciences, 18*:1342, 1976.
46. McDermott, Barry: The glitter has gone. *Sports Illustrated, 57*(2):94, November 8, 1982.
47. McNurlen, Carolyn, A.: Anorexia nervosa: is the family to blame? Can the family help? *Better Homes and Gardens*, 68d, May 1985.
48. Minuchin, S., Rosman, B. L., Baker, L.: *Psychosomatic families: Anorexia Nervosa in Context*, 6th ed., Cambridge, Harvard University Press, 1982.
49. Mitchell, Diane: Anorexia nervosa. *Arts in Psychotherapy, 7*(1):57, 1980.
50. Moldofsky, H., and Garfinkel, P. E.: Problems of treatment of anorexia nervosa. *Canadian Psychiatric Association Journal, 19*:169, 1974.
51. Monte, P. M., McCrady, B. S., Barlow, D. H.: Effect of positive reinforcement: informational feedback and contingency contracting on bulimic anorexia females. *Behavior Therapy, 8*(2):258, March 1977.
52. Papalla, Anthony and Bode, Jacqueline: Perspectives on the anorectic student. *Journal of College Student Personnel*:224-228, May 1981.
53. Piazza, E., Piazza, N., and Rollins, N.: Anorexia nervosa: controversial aspects of therapy. *Comprehensive Psychiatry, 21*(3):178, May/June 1980.
54. Pierloot, R., Vandereycken, W., Verhaest, S.: An inpatient treatment program for anorexia nervosa patients. *Acta Psychiatrica Scandinavia, 66*(1):7, July 1982.
55. Polivy, Janet: *Group Therapy for Anorexia Nervosa*. Toronto, University of Toronto and Clarke Institute of Psychiatry, 1979, pp. 1.

56. Pertschuk, M. J., Forster, J., Buzby, G., and Mullen, J. L.: The treatment of anorexia nervosa with total parenteral nutrition. *Biological Psychiatry, 167*(6):540, June 1981.

57. Rodin, Judith: A sense of control. *Psychology Today,* December 1984, pp. 43.

58. Romeo, Felicia F.: Anorexia nervosa: sociological considerations for the private practitioners. *Psychotherapy in Private Practice, 1*(3), Fall 1983.

59. Romeo, Felicia F.: *Women, Anorexia Nervosa, and Culture, Delta Kappa Gamma Bulletin, 49*(2), Winter 1983.

60. Romeo, Felicia F.: The physical educator and anorexia nervosa. *The Physical Educator, 41*(1), March 1984.

61. Romeo, Felicia F.: Anorexia nervosa in the middle school. *The Middle School Journal, IV*(4), August 1984.

62. Romeo, Felicia F.: Adolescence, sexual conflict and anorexia nervosa. *Adolescence,* Fall 1984.

63. Romeo, Felicia F.: Early identification of anorexia nervosa in the classroom *The High School Journal, 67*(2), December/January 1984.

64. Ross, Jack L.: Anorexia nervosa: an overview. *Bulletin of the Menninger Clinic, 41*(5):419, September 1977.

65. Russell, Gerald: Bulimia nervosa: an ominous variant of anorexia nervosa. *Psychological Medicine, 9*:437, 447, 1979.

66. Russell, Gerald: The current treatment of anorexia nervosa. *British Journal of Psychiatry, 138*:165, 1981.

67. Schwarz, D. M., Thompson, M. G., and Johnson, C. L.: Anorexia nervosa and bulimia: the social-cultural context. *International Journal of Eating Disorders, 1*(3):25, 319, 320, Spring 1982.

68. See, Carolyn: Anorexia nervosa is starvation by choice. *Today's Health*:50, May 1975.

69. Seligmann, J., Zabarsky, M., Witherspoon, D., Rotenbeck, L., and Schmidt, Mireya: A deadly feast and famine. *Newsweek, 60,* March 7, 1983.

70. Shiner, Gail: Anorexia nervosa studied at several centers. *Research Resources Reporter, IV*:6, May 1980.

71. Singer, Jerome E., and Krantz, David S.: Perspectives on the interface between psychology and public health. *American Psychologist, 37*(8):959, August 1982.

72. Sours, J. A.: The anorexia nervosa syndrome: physnomenologic and psychodynamic components. *Psychiatric Quarterly, 43*:240, 1969.

73. Sours, John A., M.D., *Starving to Death in a Sea of Objects.* New York, Jason Arson, 1980, pp. 187.

74. Stern, Judith S.: Weight control programs. Wynick, Myron: *Nutritional Disorders of Women,* New York, Wiley and Sons, 1977, pp. 137.

75. Strober, Michael: The significance of bulimia in juvenile anorexia nervosa: an exploration of possible etiologic factors. *International Journal of Eating Disorders, 1*(1):41, Fall 1981.

76. Swift, William J.: The long-term outcome of early onset anorexia nervosa: a critical review. *Journal of the American Academy of Child Psychiatry, 21*(1):45, January 1985. From Greenfield, N.: *Personal Communication,* 1980.

77. Thompson, Michael G., and Schwartz, Donald M.: Life adjustment of women with anorexia nervosa and anorexic-like behavior. *International Journal of Eating Disorders, 1*(2):58, Winter 1982.

78. Werry, J. S., and Bull, D.: Anorexia nervosa: a case study using behavior therapy. *Journal of American Academy of Child Psychiatry, 14*(4):648, Autumn 1975.

79. Wesley, Myrna M., Ruddy, R. D., and Ruddy, Susan, G.: Anorexia nervosa: an obsession with thinness. *Forecast for Home Economics*:119, September 1981.

80. Whipple, Stephen B., and Manning, Donald E.: Anorexia nervosa: commitment to a multifaceted treatment program. *Psychotherapy and Psychosomatics, 30*(3-4):167, 1978.

81. Winick, Myron, M.D.: *Nutrition in Health and Disease,* New York, Wiley and Sons, 1980, pp. 21.

82. Wooley, O. Wayne, and Wooley, Susan: The Beverly Hills eating disorder: the mass marketing of anorexia nervosa. *International Journal of Eating Disorders, 11*(3):67, Spring 1982.

83. Yager, Joel: Family issues in the pathogenesis of anorexia nervosa. *Psychosomatic Medicine, 44*(1):44, March 1982.

INDEX

93